The Paradigm That Changed My Life Forever

The Moment of Change

Marie M. A. Wilson- Newman

authorHOUSE

AuthorHouse™ UK
1663 Liberty Drive
Bloomington, IN 47403 USA
www.authorhouse.co.uk
Phone: UK TFN: 0800 0148641 (Toll Free inside the UK)
UK Local: (02) 0369 56322 (+44 20 3695 6322 from outside the UK)

© 2022 Marie M. A. Wilson- Newman. All rights reserved.

No part of this book may be reproduced, stored in a retrieval system, or transmitted by any means without the written permission of the author.

Published by AuthorHouse 07/25/2022

ISBN: 978-1-5462-8670-7 (sc)
ISBN: 978-1-5462-8671-4 (hc)
ISBN: 978-1-5462-8669-1 (e)

Print information available on the last page.

Any people depicted in stock imagery provided by Getty Images are models, and such images are being used for illustrative purposes only.
Certain stock imagery © Getty Images.

This book is printed on acid-free paper.

Because of the dynamic nature of the Internet, any web addresses or links contained in this book may have changed since publication and may no longer be valid. The views expressed in this work are solely those of the author and do not necessarily reflect the views of the publisher, and the publisher hereby disclaims any responsibility for them.

FOREWORD

This book represents Marie's reflections on her journey so far in her life. It has been no ordinary life, and there is no doubt that her strong personality and endurance have helped her to achieve what she has. From Jamaica to the USA to the UK, she talks through some life-changing experiences that have influenced the way she thinks and the way she lives her life.

She has travelled across continents and settled in the UK, where, as a woman of colour, she has overcome challenges and prejudice to complete her education and excel in what she does. It is a story that inspires, but also reminds us that life can throw significant challenges our way. Her account gives hope and encouragement that with persistence and self-belief, one can achieve many things.

—Dr Simon Edwards

In Marie Newman's autographical book, she shares candid personal experiences and reflections of her journey to become a nurse and an educator. Her story role-models inspiration, motivation, grace and resilience. This book will be very relevant for students and professional colleagues alike.

—Dr Julia Minoia Riches
Doctor of Nursing Practice

This book is very interesting and maps Marie's journey beautifully and should be extremely inspirational for anyone reading it.

—Dr JG

ACKNOWLEDGEMENTS

Many persons were inspirational in the completion of this book. I would like to say special thanks to:

- God for giving me the strength and courage to carry on
- My children—Seon, my musician; Shellee, my lawyer; Andre, my artist and philosophical soul; Zarya, my teacher; and Xeena, my actress. These heroes kept the momentum going.
- Euthan Newman for allowing me to be me. I found hidden strength when the notion was for me to either swim or drown.
- My parents, especially my father, who said to me, "Life is not going to be easy." I only

understood this when I was faced with circumstances that forced me to do so.

- My mother, whom I applaud for her belief in faith, grace, and hope. She called my husband Faith; our Honda car, she referred to as Grace; and myself, she called Hope. It is my deep regret that my parents are no longer here to be acknowledged personally. Selfishly, I took the early part of my life for granted, and now I wished my actions were different.
- Mr Earl Christian, the phenomenal principal who is the reason behind this education paradigm that changed my life forever
- Mr Brent Harris, my geography teacher at Titchfield High School, who always referred to me as "little genius"
- Dr Jill Geal, former principal lecturer, Bucks New University, for supporting me in completing my master's in education and for taking her precious time to read this episode

- Dr Julia Minoia Riches, former senior lecturer, Bucks New University, for believing in me and acknowledging my work
- Margaret Rioga, associate professor, Bucks New University, for her inspiration
- My family and my special friends, who helped me to keep focus
- Paula Webber and Jacqueline Ahmed, for your support
- Dr Clement Lambert, who asked me, "What are you doing with your life now?" I replied, "Working as a nurse in the UK and doing a top-up degree." He said: "What? You must be joking! I've just finished my PhD, and you used to help me in high school. You should at least have your masters by now."

PREFACE

This book has been compiled and written with privilege and purpose by author Marie Newman. It provides snapshots of the contributing factors to a personal, educational, professional, social, and spiritual journey. The book explores different encounters with regards to good times as well as the challenges faced and how these challenges were cultivated and resolved.

On the morning of May 5, 1999, I arrived in the United Kingdom, having travelled from Norman Manley International Airport, Jamaica, West Indies. The plane landed at Heathrow International Airport during the early hours of the morning. I had left four of my children--three daughters and one son—with my husband in Jamaica, and my youngest daughter was in the United States of America with my mother.

The difficult conversations and situations that I had avoided were unfolding. Instead of embracing my situation, I allowed it to become my worst long disaster. I did not have a voice, so I could not be heard.

Clement, my friend to whom I referred earlier, commented on my future educational development. This made me to reflect on past aspirations, where I wanted to be as well as the real reason I had migrated. I was able to draw from my embedded aspirations through a constructive interaction and push when Clement asked me, "What are you doing with your life now?"

This took me back to the experience I had with the principal's (Mr Earl Christian's) paradigm. It did not seem significant to me at the time, yet this turned out to be the greatest paradigm.

INTRODUCTION

This book shares my narrative and reflections on the support network and resources that helped me achieved dreams I never knew would be a reality. There are highlights of some special persons, including the teachers who encouraged me to strive for excellence in education, which is now of great significance to me. The early beginnings, the learning, and the significance of continuous belief in self are discussed.

The book focuses on a true story, from a humble start with the principal's paradigm to the developmental steps of becoming a nurse, a ward manager, a team leader, a senior practitioner, a practice educator, and a university senior lecturer. The journey demonstrates how faith, hope, grace, determination, support, and hard work provided opportunities that evolved not only from the paradigm but from the principal who believed in me and some true heroes who were a part of this journey.

WHY AM I ONLY JUST PUBLISHING THIS BOOK?

Finally, after twenty-two years of conceptualizing, this book has become a reality. The delay in its completion was due to the many challenges, twists, and turns along the journey. Each year, I changed the timeline, as I tried to convince myself that I would at last be completing the book. My procrastination, family demands, prioritizing of others' needs, and dearth of motivation put the brake on my drive to finalise this manuscript for publication.

I told many persons that I was writing a book. Some said that they wanted to venture into writing as well. Their books were finished and published, and yet my malingering attitude persisted for years on end. Whilst it was easy saying that I *will* write this book, it was a difficult task taking it through to the end. I could not keep the motivation going to do the final manuscript, even with the goals and the repeated New Year's resolutions I had set myself.

I was emotionally tormented by the lack of support that I thought I needed, both physically and emotionally, especially when I did not see the happily-ever-after life I had anticipated. My motivation fluctuated as I stopped and started writing over a thousand times. Even after submission and paying the publishing company, it took me years to confirm the final agreement for publication.

When my inspiration was high, I worked as if there was no tomorrow, only to be cut off again as the stalling crept up and overpowered me. This is a feeling that is difficult to explain. I was trapped in my own created world, with the constant thoughts and beliefs that I had to be the support for my family. Worthy of noting was that this happened countless times, and often I could not understand the source of the setback. There was nothing physically holding me back; it was my own thoughts, and this is what I failed to see.

There were occasions when I even thought that completing the book was not going to be possible, as I could not keep focus no matter how I tried. I juggled between procrastination and motivation for a very long time. I strongly believe now that these setbacks provided different opportunities of learning for me that I was too preoccupied to take note of.

I look back now with pride, as without the challenges, I would probably still be the naïve girl believing that everyone means well. I was described by many as *petite and cannot mash ants* (Jamaican parlance for being totally harmless). I trusted and believed that what people said they would do, they would do. Therefore, when I asked for help from the people, I consider to be close friends and family, I failed to accept that this was not going to be possible.

It is not a give-to-get, but sometimes you find yourself in situations. For example, like the widow's mite, I gave my last two thousand dollars to someone when I saw a need, yet, when I needed one dollar, there was no reciprocity. I was fooling the one person I should believe in most, which was myself.

For many years, I blamed myself for being foolish by working selflessly and not being able to believe or do otherwise. I recall my supervisor, Sister Satchell, telling me one day that "There is so much in being kind and so much in being a fool." Some of the biggest erudition curves came from when I shared my ideas and plans with people, I thought were close, yet this ended with even more disappointment. The responsibility was on me to seek and find the right resources.

The premise of this book came solely from these complex but factual experiences. The main thing lacking in my life was not how to take care of others. It was how to prioritize my needs and take care of my own well-being and my personal and professional development.

CHAPTER 1

EARLY BEGINNINGS

My mother was keen for her children to have a good education. I was less than the required age for primary school, yet my mother insisted on sending me to school.

Doctors said I was frail, and they were doubtful about my future. Both on the journey to school or at school, there were older schoolmates who took an interest in ensuring my safety. I am grateful to my schoolmates, especially Millie, whose mother was one of our two caretakers. Millie would carry my school bag, and she often carried me on her back.

It was difficult to walk the long route to school without taking breaks. Sometimes on these breaks, we would stop to pick mangoes from the trees by the roadside. A good supply of seasonal mangoes was a special treat from Millie. I enjoyed eating green mangoes coated in brown sugar as we walked the long, lonely road home after school in the evenings.

The main road leading to my school was stony, slippery, and at times muddy, especially after any rainfall. The dangers we encountered are unbelievable looking back. With the slightest slip in certain places, one could easily end up over a precipice. As schoolchildren, we would sometimes push boundaries without being aware of risks, despite warnings from our parents.

My sister Prachin was reported by a passer-by to our parents for walking on the wall bordering Viaduct Bridge, Fruitful Vale District, Portland, on her way home from school. Just looking over this bridge is a danger, more so walking on its walls. Looking over the bridge made me feel like gravity was pulling me over.

My cousin B sustained a fractured arm after she fell into a gully whilst we were taking turns swinging over a precipice one evening after school. Swinging over these gullies was great fun at the time, and none of us children took any notice of the risks. If I could relive my life, I would probably think twice before venturing into such fun but dangerous activities.

On the way to and from school, I walked up bumps and hills. By the time I got to my destination, I was tired. If Mr Christian knew what we went through to even reach school, he would have probably reconsidered many disciplinary actions, as rarely was being late the least of our problems.

The school was a wooden structure on the corner of the long stretch of road in Cooper's Hill Square, Portland, Jamaica. My uncles, Fetchy or Bentley, would sometimes take us on their motorbike to school to ensure we got there on time. Looking back at this, four children on a motorbike was a dangerous behaviour—but awesome!

My youngest sister, Michelle, was ill from birth. Having been diagnosed with a heart condition, she was given a poor prognosis by her cardiologist. The family's focus was on Michelle's health. As a family, we were all devastated by this sad news. The saying "don't throw away what is not dead" fits well here. With the diligent care from our aunt Jenny, salt-bath treatments, and continuous appointments at the Bustamante Hospital for Children, the total body oedema gradually subsided over time. A significant note is that Michelle now works as a registered nurse in a prominent hospital in the United States of America, giving back the care that was once given to her.

My two older brothers, Ken and Geoffery, and my eldest sister, Carol, lived in boarded accommodation in the capital city of Portland, Jamaica, known as Port Antonio, where they attended high and secondary schools. At the time, there was no regular bus route from our village to the town. Hence, my parents had to find accommodation in town for the kids to get a good education.

I suffered from asthma, a respiratory illness, from childhood, which often required medical intervention. I would become unwell due to allergies and changes in weather conditions. As a result of the illness, my parents were always protective of me. This made my siblings call me "the pet."

Denny, one of my cousins, bought me a medicine called Liqufruta to help with the fits of coughing. Despite its repugnant taste, it had good effect combined with the Ventolin therapy and my father's home-made herbal remedies.

The swishing sound of the trees coupled with the shrieking sounds of birds were familiar noises that echoed on our farm and woke me up every morning. I could hear my mother in the background saying, "It's four o'clock; it's time to get up." She would repeatedly say this until everyone was awake.

It was intriguing to watch the chickens and roosters as they nestled themselves on the branches of the nearby trees in the evenings to go off to sleep. On waking up in the early hours of the morning, I would hear the familiar singing of the birds and crowing of the roosters: *cock-a-doodle-doo, cock-a-doodle-doo.* The early morning breeze meandered through the half-open windows. In those days, it was safe to leave our windows and doors open even when not at home. Now I would be cautious doing this.

The air was cool and fresh; the grass and flowers were wet with dew. Family worship started the day's activities, followed by my home chores and helping my father with work on the farm. The smell of fresh fever grass was refreshing as I cut it to feed the animals. The chickens were fed corn that was picked on the farm. The corn was sun-dried and crushed in a mortar using a pestle. Some of the chickens were raised in coops and others were allowed to be free range on the farm.

We lived on a hilly farmland, which was a scene to behold—especially standing by the banks that overlooked the green pastures watching the cows and goats nibbling at the carpeted grassland. I shared a bedroom with my sister Ve when all nine siblings were at home during school holidays. However, when our other siblings were at their boarded accommodation in Port Antonio, we could choose any room we wanted to occupy. Disagreements with my sister during the day were short-lived, as by bedtime we were best friends again as we negotiated among ourselves who slept where on the bed.

It was fascinating, the things we did as children. What does it matter who sleeps on which side of the bed? Even in adult life, when we go on holiday, my sister still wants first choice of where to sleep if we share the same room. These habits were easy to adopt but hard to change. Some things changed naturally over time, some I made a conscious effort to change, and some never changed at all.

Ve appeared more conscientious, as she seemed to manage chores and school life better than I did. She acted more mature than her age; she took everything seriously and did not seem to find jokes as funny as I did. When I was laughing, my sister often asked me, "What is so funny? What is the joke about?" Often, I was unable to explain the joke to her. On the other hand, my sister Janelle had a good sense of humor. She would join in readily with laughter with any joke shared with her. Even with the same parents, and same upbringing we were all different.

My school holidays were spent in Port Antonio or Kingston, Jamaica, with family and friends, or on the farm doing chores, such as milking cows and goats, preparing food for the animals, picking fruits, shelling peas, and the list goes on. Particularly, I enjoyed going for a horseback ride with my sister Ve. I helped wash the green bananas; pick cocoa and coffee beans; and pack the boxes for export. Sometimes we picked ripened pods of cocoa for ourselves, as the beans had a particular sweetish taste when taken fresh from the pods.

At the time, I thought this was such a terrible life, living on the farm, being awakened every day by the same noise of birds, caring for the animals, and looking at the forestry in the distance. I always wished my parents would move to live in the town area. When I asked my parents about this, some of the responses given were "We do not want to live too close to the town or coastline in case of a tsunami" or "The air is fresher in the countryside—in the last days, people will crave to move to the countryside."

It was not until my parents passed away that I realized that this was the best part of my life—more so now that it is gone. I smile at the memories now, knowing that whilst living on our parents' farm, we were our own bosses. Yet as a child, I never appreciated this. I now take special pride in knowing that we never had to watch our backs or worry about others' perceptions or claims.

There were workers both on the farm and in the house, yet I did not escape from being given my share of duties to perform. Respect was of paramount importance, and all adults, regardless of their job or status or class, were referred to as *miss, mistress,* or *mister.* The expectation from my parents was for me to share a polite greeting with every adult with whom I came in contact. If this was not adhered to and a report was made to my mother or father, I had to prepare myself for parental disciplinary measures.

Food products reaped from the farm for export purpose were screened thoroughly for size, fitness, insect bites, spots, or marks, yet at times there were still some rejections. These were mainly green bananas, which my father packed in a drum for ripening to feed the animals. Often, I would help my father run the old-fashioned homemade juice mill to manually squeeze the sugarcane to make sugarcane juice.

This was something I looked forward to doing, as I watched the juice drain through the funnel into the collecting container. I enjoyed having a glass of ice-cold sugarcane juice along with chunks of dry coconut or coconut jelly with scoops of the wet dark-coloured cane sugar that was made by my grandfather. Those were some of the things that I found pleasurable whilst growing up.

As I humbled myself, I came to accept that it was not property, a big house, top job, or money that was important; it was a joyous feeling to be in the company of supportive, caring genuine people and enjoying nature at its best. The common phrase used in Jamaica was "no problem." This meant that if there was a problem, a resolution was at hand. Having my parents around was indeed a blessing and a privilege that I took for granted for many years.

CHAPTER 2

THE ABSENT PARENT

My parents were not around at separate intervals for a part of my early years growing up. My father, who was away for much longer than my mother, had migrated to North America. His absence left a gap in our family that no one could fill. Even though we received regular mail from him, it was not the same as him being at home.

In one of the letters, he wrote, "They are killing people here for one cent." My mother would pray every day for his safety. I missed my dad, as life without him was not as kind as when he was around.

During his absence, our home was used to accommodate some of our extended family. My mother was running a grocery store and a dressmaking business, so we were mainly left in the care of the housekeepers, Ms Selma and Miss Audrey.

The care was much different compared to when my father was at home. My father made good provision for the home, and we felt safe when he was present. My mother, though caring in her own world, was strict, always working, and never appeared to have much work-life balance. On her day off on a Saturday, she took us to church from nine in the morning until sunset. Evening time was closed by singing the song, "Now the day is over, night is drawing nigh, shadows of the evening still across the sky, now the darkness gathers …"

It was routine for my mother to give us up to thirteen Bible verses to study and recite from memory at church. My mother made sure that I was available, at any last-minute call, to fit into the sabbath (Saturday) church programme. I dared not decline any responsibilities given to me. I had to recite poems, sing solos, and take a lead role in the young people's department within the church. Another task was to deliver home-cooked food to elderly house-bound people after school, even before I had my own dinner.

On Sundays, my mother spent most of the day sewing, as she had deadlines to meet in her dressmaking duties. This made me miss my father even more. I helped my mother with hemming dresses and skirts and matching materials to make patchwork bed linen and floor mats to meet the demand and supply needs of the community.

My father returned home after what felt like a century living in the United States of America. We all went to the airport on a chartered family outing to celebrate his return. The family was all excited to have him back, and things gradually went back to normal.

One of the stories my father shared regarding his job in North America was that when he was offered a job working in the iron and steel industry, he had no clue what the job was about. He accepted the job and learned to do it during his orientation. He said that education cannot be underestimated, but common sense was the key in his development.

CHAPTER 3

PRIMARY-SCHOOL LIFE

I started school in a grade one with a few children who were a little older than I was. This may have been part of the reason it took me a longer time than others to adjust to the new school routines. Learning was great fun, and although shyness overshadowed me in the initial phase, I was always quiet, polite, and respectful in and out of class. I dared not do otherwise, as this would put me at the mercy of my mother if she received any reports.

The Monday to Friday journey to school was the norm, rain or shine. Regardless of the reason, there was no excuse that I could think of that could keep my mother from sending me to school. One of the senior girls always carried my school bag. My schoolmates took turns carrying me on their backs.

Krissy was one of my close friends. Ve and I often visited her house after school. We would stop at the local shop, owned by Krissy's grandmother, to buy homemade biscuit and cheese and strawberry-syrup iced lollies. After school, I enjoyed picking the traditional fruits, such as gimbilin and mangoes. I must mention one of my morning and evening tasks of searching for basacom (these were little green berries that I found to be very tasty) through the grass field close by Coopers Hill School.

School was superb. Each day brought on new challenges and excitement. Ms Cynthia, my grade-one teacher, was caring and compassionate towards me. In the initial phase of starting school during break period, I just stood far off and watched others play. I never participated in the games. The main games played were ball games and skipping.

I did not join in the games for two main reasons. First, my mother had given me strict warnings to avoid playing with others, as she did not want to hear of any incidents or complaints. Second, I did not know how to play these games.

I felt a little left out just watching the games, so one day I decided to join in. The skipping rope always ended up slapping on my feet and bruising my legs, as I was not jumping fast enough. When I reached home, my mother questioned how this happened and reinforced her previous warnings.

Is teaching only about classroom work? For Ms Cynthia, classroom work was only one aspect of teaching and learning. During break time, Ms Cynthia, having observed that I was not engaging in the games, came to the play field to help me get involved. She skipped with me in her arms, and she taught me how to skip and gave me the right timing of when to jump. It did not take long for me to learn to play skip.

Soon, I was having fun playing, even though I was still a bit timid. As a result of this, I carefully selected who I played with, in keeping with my mother's warning to keep safe and avoid activities that could exacerbate an asthma attack.

It was during this period that my sister Alison went to live with an aunty who was the postwoman for the community. Due to the move, Alison was now attending a different school from us, her siblings. Alison would cry whenever she visited us and it was time for her to go home. My mother thought this was best for Alison, as Aunty did not have any children of her own, and being the only child in that household, she thought that Alison would be well cared for. However, this was not the case, as my sister not only disliked living away from her real parents and her siblings but hated living with Aunty.

I would give Alison gifts and toys to cheer her up when she visited. Despite this, she was angry and upset, and although she took the gifts, this did not seem to help the situation. I could not seem to soothe the situation no matter what I did. What I laughed at made my sister cry. I should have respected her views and her situation even if we had different perspectives, but I lacked cognition in this area at the time.

When she was 13 years old, Alison returned home to live with us and attend Titchfield High School. I cannot say if Alison ever moved on from her past years of temporary foster life. She still talks about this as if it were yesterday. The emotions of these experiences have lingered for a long time, and this impacted on me as a sibling, I often asked why this even happened in the first place. Looking back, I believe it is crucial to be positive around children, as there is a tendency that similar traits can be developed, with lasting impact.

CHAPTER 4

MR CHRISTIAN

My primary school employed a new principal named Mr Christian. He took over as head of the school, and his wife, Mrs Christian, taught first grade. My teachers were all different; they taught their lessons using their own special teaching and learning style. Each teacher I encountered left a unique feeling. No two teachers were the same, yet each was effective and efficient in one way or another.

One morning, the principal, Mr Christian, came to my class unannounced. Usually when the principal visited a class in such a manner, there was a problem regarding non-compliance with school rules and regulations. Today seemed different, as instead of warnings about school rules and expectations, Mr Christian gave the class a math problem to work on. He gave all attendees equal opportunity to answer the question. He asked us students one at a time to give the answer to the math question.

My classmates were calling out their answers, such as: *one, two, three, four, five, six, seven,* and the list went on, as some students reiterated answers that were given before. When it was my

turn to answer, I said 0.5. Mr Christian asked me
to repeat the answer, and I did: 0.5.

At the end of the question-and-answer session, Mr Christian looked at me and nodded his head. I couldn't make sense of the look on his face. He said firmly, "Marie, at lunchtime, meet me in my office."

He walked briskly out of the classroom and went towards his office. I watched him as he disappeared around the corner. I sat in the classroom wondering why I had to go to the principal's office. He never said if my answer was right or wrong. Mixed feelings and various questions occupied my thoughts, as well as fear of what the meeting with Mr Christian was about.

I became more and more anxious as lunchtime drew nearer. I thought: *Am I in trouble? What did I do or say wrong? Why is the principal asking me to come to his office at lunchtime? Why not someone else?* Ideas of all sorts raced through my head as I repeatedly ask myself, *Why me?* Palpitations kicked in as the clock ticked away closer and closer to the noon hour.

Mr Christian had informed me at the start of the school term that my job was to look out for students who suck their fingers and to report this back to him. I never reported anyone to Mr

Christian. I could not do so, as my sister Ve and I were the only two students in the institution who sucked our fingers. I started thinking that the reason for the summons to his office could be linked to me sucking my fingers, as I was often caught out doing this. Therefore, my initial thoughts were that I was called in for disciplinary measures relating to this.

At exactly twelve noon, the bell rang for lunch break. In keeping with Pavlovian classical conditioning theory, at the sound of the bell, my classmates rushed to join the line for their cooked school lunch. I timidly walked through the small corridor towards the principal's office, which was adjacent to my classroom. I knocked on the blue door hoping that the principal would not be in, but his firm tone came ringing back: "Come in."

I walked into the office, and Mr Christian instructed me to take a seat. He looked at me sternly, then with a little smile on his face handed me a list of mathematics questions to complete. Surprisingly, no questions were asked about the job I was given to report students who sucked their fingers. This was a relief for me.

I sat in silence and worked my way diligently through the questions until I was finished. It did not take me too long. I still had time to get some lunch before the break was up. I handed the completed answer sheet to Mr Christian, and as I turned to leave his office, he said, "Come back tomorrow at the same time."

This pattern repeated itself. Every day at lunchtime, I would meet with Mr Christian for extra classes in mathematics and English. I was left in suspense; there was absolutely no indication of what this was about. Mr Christian may have been looking for a student to represent the school, but he never declared that I was being prepared for an examination. Mr Christian was full of new ideas for the school's development.

Finally, the day came when Mr Christian informed me that he had recommended for me to sit for the Jamaica Ministry of Education Common Entrance Examination. I was one of the first students from this institution to have the privilege of doing this prestigious examination.

Oh! What a privilege, what a joy divine, when someone cares. They will find a way to help you, as Mr Christian did in this life-changing case.

CHAPTER 5

THE TEACHER'S IMPACT

My teachers had the greatest influence on my learning, whether positive or otherwise. This sometimes made me do better and other times made me do worse. My views during those early years were vastly different from my current perspective. My feelings were dependent on my thinking as well as my interpretation of the teaching and learning experiences.

I had several different teachers throughout my school life. Mrs Christian became my new grade-one teacher after Miss Cynthia resigned. Miss Lyn taught me one semester. She was always smiling, had the most unique handwriting, and always had a kind word to say. She took much interest in supporting her students.

Festus Campbell, a teacher in his own unique way, always had a complimentary phrase to say. He kept in contact with me even after he left the school. He became an author and migrated to England. Every time Festus published a book, he would write me a letter instructing me to get a copy from Sangster's Bookstore in downtown Kingston, Jamaica. The last contact with Mr Campbell that I can recall was in the early 1980s; he sent me a card, and I have still never figured out what he meant. I read the card several times to make sense of the written words.

The card read: "Who we are and who we become is determined by those who love us." To me, this had many meanings, and on the other hand, it could be based on one's own interpretation. In one light, this could only have been a good gesture. I discussed and shared these books with my sister

Ve, who said she often wondered if Festus was referring to us in his books, as the writings were related to some of the experiences in our early childhood education when he was her teacher.

Mrs Hardy was my grade-two teacher as well as my school mother. Her daughter Verna, who was also on the teaching staff, became a true shoulder to lean on. I spent many weekends and holidays with Mrs Hardy and her family in the Teachers' Cottage at Coopers Hill School and at her home in Norwich, Portland. She never made me feel any different from her family. I was treated the same as her own children, and they too treated me like family. She always gave her students a packet of Shirley biscuit as a favourite treat.

CHAPTER 6

STAYING OVERNIGHT AT THE TEACHER'S COTTAGE

One evening, my sisters and I stayed back to play on the school grounds after school. We played for hours, not paying attention to the time and not realizing that it was getting late. It became dark without us taking any notice, and suddenly nightfall started to set in. It was now too late to travel home on our own, as it was not safe to do so in the dark.

My sister Carol made the decision that we should stay over for the night at the teachers' cottage with one of our teachers, Mrs Hardy. My father was not aware of this. The decision was made solely by my sister without informing my father. We took no note of our actions, as we were all enjoying the fun time.

My mother was living abroad at the time, and we were left in the care of my father and the housekeepers, Miss Audrey and Miss Selma. Miss Selma, though caring towards me, always seemed to pick on my sister Ve. One day, I watched her run behind Ve with a broom in her hand. She was threatening to beat Ve with the broomstick, which was scary.

My father and the housekeeper, Miss Selma, had prepared us for school on the day we decided to stay back for extracurricular activities. We were always expected to be home by the latest five in the evening after school. Today was different, as we did not go home.

I was awakened up from sleep by my father's familiar voice calling, "Mrs Hardy, Mrs Hardy." At first it was like a dream. I heard the familiar whinnying sounds of my father's horse. The loud neighing of the horse continued for a while.

I pulled back the window curtains to see what was happening. My father rode his horse in the wee hours of the night; he was still sitting in the saddle when I went out to greet him by the porch. A tired-looking distraught father's glossy eyes stared back at me as he held onto the reins whilst the horse kept moving its head in a ringing motion from side to side. I could see how hurt he was, yet my gut feeling was that, though feeling hurt, he was happy to see us—more so, to know that we were safe.

He looked at me and shook his head. I could see the tears welling up in his eyes. My father had come looking for us, his children. We had no idea at the time of the impact our behaviour had on a lone parent at home.

Mrs Hardy said, "Come in, Mr Wilson."

My father's very emotional and saddened deep tone came back. "I can't come in, Mrs Hardy."

Mrs Hardy then asked him, "Why, Mr Wilson?"

He said, "My heart is too full, Mrs Hardy. I came home from work and was told by the housekeeper that my children did not come home from school. I was so worried."

I felt petrified, not being sure of the consequences of our actions. But most of all, I shared my father's emotional pain. How could we have been so horrible to our father? He was a great father to us, and we knew he loved us. What were we thinking?

I can only imagine what this must have felt like for my father. Although tired from a hard day's work, and distraught and disappointed at our behaviour, my father was happy to take us home. He bundled up all four of us on the horse's back. He thanked Mrs Hardy for looking after us. We told Miss Hardy goodbye and left to make our way home. As the horse trotted along the dark lonely road, we held tightly around each other's waist for support.

From this scenario, I learned to challenge decisions that do not seem right. I now know that I can ask why, when, where, how, and what without being seen as disrespectful. My mother thought it was confrontational to do so and expected us children to be seen but not heard. This type of upbringing seemed to lend itself to the characteristics of humbleness, putting others first, and listening rather than talking. This was often misinterpreted as passive.

My eldest sister Carol had told us it was OK to stay over and sleep for the night. We could have challenged her, yet none of us siblings did. Until I had similar experiences with my own children, I was not able to say how it felt for my father when his children did not come home from school—more so, not knowing the whereabouts of his children. What was simple and seemed like a joke to us was taken very seriously by our father. It was evident that our behaviours were emotionally draining for him too.

CHAPTER 7

THE PLAN TO MIGRATE

My Aunt Una was working as a bank manager in the Bahamas. The plan was for my sister Ve and I to migrate from Jamaica to the Bahamas to live with Aunt Una. We had a great send-off party. Our suitcases were packed and everything was ready, including travel documents—except for the plane tickets that were expected to arrive by the post. The tickets finally came at the last minute. My mother, interpreting things her way when the delivery of the tickets was delayed, cancelled the travel plans abruptly, as she thought someone was trying to sabotage our trip. As the weeks, months, and years rolled by, I eventually forgot about any plans to migrate.

One day, we were visited by an aunt from Canada who asked for my sister Ve and I to live in Canada with her. My mother decided that it would be best for our cousin Laurel to travel with my sister, as she was older, and they would be good support for each other.

It was a gloomy, quiet day in 1973, with mild drizzling rain. I heard the familiar engine of the chartered green Jeep my father had booked to take Ve and Laurel to the airport. The driver came out of the vehicle and was standing in the driveway waiting for the girls to board the transport. Tears ran down my cheeks. It was difficult to control my feelings.

My thoughts were, *How could my sister be even thinking of leaving me behind?* Ve did not ask why I was not coming with her, and she did not say goodbye. She and Laurel were all dressed up, both wearing their green crimpling pantsuits that my mother had made for them. I felt betrayed and deprived as I watched them do the final preparation before leaving.

Overwhelmed with sad feelings that my sister was leaving, I was uncertain of how I was going to cope. I was losing my sister, my confidant, my twin, my best friend, and it was too much to bear. Even when the send-off party was in full swing, with everyone eating and drinking, I looked to see what my sister was doing. She showed no visible emotion.

I looked back at the bad times as well as the good times. I did not want to lose my sister after all we had been through. We had been inseparable all our lives, not spending a single night without each other. I did not want to let go. Everyone in our community called us the twin girls, and most persons thought we were twins, although this was not the case. We were simply siblings from the same parents.

Despite the symbiosis, our views and perceptions were different. This made me realize that feelings and ideas can differ even among close relations. I had to stop believing that friends or family would think in the same way. It was often each to one's own.

Different scenes were relived in my head, such as when we were burnt by hot water and taken to hospital. We were both under 10 years old when my sister and I tried to cook a meal in the absence of our parents. We were copying what we saw the housekeepers doing, as they always had a meal prepared when my parents arrived home from work.

I was giving advice to my sister that the water was boiling. She thought differently, and while we were both peeking over the pot to confirm this, it fell from the coal stove, spilling the hot water all over our bodies. We were both hospitalized for treatment. I believe children should not be left alone without adequate supervision. As children, we did not know the dangers that we were putting ourselves in despite all the best intentions.

My sister's luggage was already packed in the back of the green Jeep. My sister and Laurel sat, seemingly comfortably, in the back of the Jeep, ready to hit the road to a foreign land. No one seemed to realize what I was going through. The focus was on getting my sister to the airport on time for her flight. I could not keep back the tears. I went under my mother's bed so I would not have to face seeing my sister leave.

Now everything I could think of meant nothing to me. I did not eat all day, and I had no appetite for food. Within a few weeks, my weight loss was becoming more evident, as I refused food and drink, day after day. Depression began and probably completed its course without any significant note taken of this. I am now more aware of low mood and the clinical manifestations associated with this, such as the lack of interest in activities that were normally enjoyable, refusing food and drink, self-neglect, and isolation.

I became thin and frail, and it came to a point where my parents were now concerned. I was taken to the doctor for assessment and treatment. Visits to the doctors became more and more regular. On each visit to Dr Antonio, he gave me blocks of chocolate wrapped in shiny silver paper. I guess this was to cheer me up somewhat.

My father, who was referred to as the "king of the forest," made home remedies from a variety of herbal plants. I was also given herbs, roots tea, cod liver oil, and a medicine I can only recall as "Scot's Emulsion." This was my regular homemade medicine when I was sick to get me well, and it was also used as a preventative therapy. Although this helped in some ways, it did not stop me from getting unwell and having to get expert medical attention. These medicines sometimes caused nausea and vomiting.

As the days, weeks, months, and years passed, I had to learn to adjust without my sister. School and home life were no longer the same.

Ve often wrote to me about her new life in Canada. We exchanged letters on a regular basis, updating each other on how we were hoping to meet up again. At the time, I had the reassurance that one day I would migrate to live with her in Canada. Her words were always reassuring, and all her letters ended with "Anyways, I am going to get you to come and live in Canada soon."

This never happened as planned, but in my later life, I was able to visit Ve in Canada. She took me on a tour of where she first lived when she moved to Canada and surprisingly shared some of her separation anxiety, most of which was comparable to my own experiences. One experience she shared was going out on the patio to cry for reasons known only to herself.

CHAPTER 8

THE AWARD CEREMONY AND THE CONFESSION

Ms Spence was one of my amazing teachers. I respected her not just for her teaching but also for her honesty, as outlined in the story that I am about to share. She was a known disciplinarian who helped to mould students' character.

The school's award ceremony was about to begin. Parents, friends, schoolmates, and teachers were all seated. Ms Spence walked up to the stage, glanced over to the area where I was sitting, then looked back at the sheet of paper she held in her hand. She began: "I don't know how to say this." Then she paused for a moment and sighed. "But

I have a confession to make." Everyone waited eagerly to hear the confession as Ms Spence chuckled and cleared her throat.

I too had no idea what Ms Spence was about to reveal as she continued her speech. Then she openly declared the following: "I marked Marie's exam papers and collated the grades. I noticed that she was in first place again. I went through each paper, and I took five points off each of the grades so that another student could get a chance to achieve first place, as Marie is always coming in first."

This was a surprise not only to me but to everyone, as they shuddered at the comment. The room fell silent. This was the last thing that I had expected—at least, not from Ms Spence, who was so strict and quick to instil discipline in us students. To deliberately reduce my exam marks to benefit another student was a point of concern, despite her good intentions. What is expected after reducing each grade by five marks?

Ms Spence said she counted the grades again one by one to make sure she had subtracted the five marks from each subject. Then she admitted, "After all the deductions, I checked the marks again, and to my disappointment Marie was still on top grade, I thought to myself, *I have to give Marie her well-earned grade.*

Ms Spence had a choice here as well. She could still take off more marks to benefit her desired student, as the ball was in her court, and who would know about this had she not mentioned it at the school awards ceremony? This to me seemed to be the irony of dignity and integrity. Ms Spence acknowledged her actions, and she made the decision to do something about it that was the right thing to do.

I was not as happy with the award as I was with Ms Spence's honesty in sharing her story. I am grateful that Ms Spence took ownership of what she did and made amends. Ms Spence said, "Marie not only came first in the class, she also came first in all subject areas. Had I taken off another five marks, she would have continued to sit in first place. This can be linked to the saying, *"What is yours will be yours."* Then she added, "I have a surprise for Marie."

At this point, Ms Spence called me to the stage to collect my gift. I was awarded for highest achievement and gained first place in the final examination. I collected the gift, shook hands with Ms Spence, and walked back to my seat. I tore a bit of the shiny wrapping paper in anticipation to see what the neatly wrapped surprise was.

The first gift I received from Ms Spence was a dictionary, and the second gift was a Bible. I could not help but wonder why Ms Spence had given me a dictionary and a Bible for my present.

The impression she had given was that the gifts were a treat and a big surprise.

It took me a while to figure out the real significance of these two books. Although I was appreciative of the award, these books were not what I had been hoping to find in the meticulously wrapped packets. However, they became two of my most valuable gifts ever received.

This whole situation helped me to develop a better mindset about what may seem simple yet can have such tremendous and valuable impact. This experience not only pointed me in the right direction, it also helped me to have a more enquiring mindset when it was needed, and I hope for this not to be mistaken for a confrontational attitude. It is only when you have walked my road that you will fully understand this.

My intention was to honour my parents for their sacrifice and hard work. As a result of this, I started looking for how to use these books in a purposeful way. I read the Bible, and I studied the dictionary. My goal was to learn a new word every day, and I practiced using these words to construct sentences to not only build my vocabulary but improve my communication skills and writing ability.

Upon reflection, this probably could have been done the other way around. Nonetheless, I benefited from both the Bible and the dictionary. To this day, I find both useful. I still have a Bible and a dictionary on my night table at home and refer to these books frequently as needed.

Words and their meanings are vital in expressions and analysis—to get the context right. Having a faith was helpful for me, as I always had something to lean on, and this helped me to uphold principles and standards, especially in my nursing career. Even though I was not perfect at everything, my philosophy was, if I could not raise my standards, I refused to lower what I already had.

The foundations built from the two books significantly helped with my understanding as well as assuring personal and academic development. Throughout my time at Cooper's Hill School, I was awarded first place every year. This was the reason Ms Spence gave for wanting to give another student a chance to achieve first place.

I learned how important it is to set goals and keep focus to remain motivated. It was imperative to believe in myself, as others could not believe in me for me. Despite this, the imperfection in me faltered along the way. There were days when I was motivated and full of confidence, and there were days when I had little or no motivation to do anything. It was a daily struggle, especially when I had to fight myself to keep focus and avoid distractions.

CHAPTER 9

THE UNEXPECTED LETTER

I was progressing through my grade-six class, and it was time to do the exam that would determine my future education—a high school or a secondary school placement. Students had to pass the common entrance examination, which was considered a scholarship by the Jamaican Board of Education to enter high school.

I stayed with my aunt Brenda in Berry Dale, a little village nearby Fellowship All Age School, where I was scheduled to sit for the common entrance examination. My mother gave me a slice of potato pudding to take with me the morning of the exam. My cousin Joan often reminded me how I threw the pudding in the rubbish bin as soon as I arrived at the exam centre that morning. The reason was, I was embarrassed for anyone to see me eating potato pudding at school. My cousin Joan said I could have offered it to her, but I was not thinking that she would have wanted the pudding either.

My father once told me, "You will pay millions for the food you waste now." I now wish I could get some of that same sweet potato pudding again. I have tried making potato pudding many times, but the taste has never been the same as that of my mother's. Currently, Jamaican sweet potato in the UK can cost between £4.99-£5.99 per kg. I am appreciative now that I cannot get back what will never be the same.

I am cognizant that when opportunity is gone, the same rarely comes back, if any at all. This goes with the notion that "Donkey don't know the use of its tail until he loses it." I should have been working and paying more attention when the sun was shining, as it is a lot more difficult to work in the rain.

Nonetheless, I sat for my common entrance examination as planned, and my initial thoughts were that it went well thanks to Mr Christian's investment in me. After a few months, I met Mrs Christian in the schoolyard. She came close to me as if she was going to greet me, but instead, she pinched my arm a couple of times. This really hurt, and at first, I had no idea why she was doing this. However, I later learnt that the examination result for those students who were successful had been published in the national newspaper. Mrs Christian was disappointed that my name was not on the published list of students who had passed the examination.

The common entrance was a high-stakes examination that determined which school Jamaican students attended. A child could be sent to a prestigious traditional high school or a non-traditional school, which was considered less prestigious. After my discussion with Mrs Christian, I started to look back to try to remember the questions and my responses. I asked myself all sorts of silly questions, such as, *Did I not put my name on my paper? Did my paper get lost? Or did I simply fail to pass the exam?*

I humbled myself and accepted that regardless of the reason, this was probably not to be. After all, no other student from the school had taken the exam before, much less passed the exam, so although I did not pass, this was not so much of a big issue. That is, until I met with my headmaster.

Mr Christian, my conscientious, dedicated, caring, passionate, phenomenal headmaster, decided to probe further into the results to find out why I was not on the list. This seemed to be such an unfortunate outcome after all his committed input. I now felt as if I had let down the school and my principal. This dedicated headmaster had devoted his time to prepare me for this exam. But Mr Christian approached me calmly and reassured me not to worry. He said that he would check with the Ministry of Education to see what went wrong.

Mr Christian kept to his word. One Saturday, during the late part of the summer period, my mother told me to go to the post office to collect her letters. I had just returned from church after a long service and was feeling tried and exhausted. I did not want to go to the post office, but I had no choice. I dared not tell my mother that I did not want to go. Reluctantly, I travelled the lonely road about a mile and a half by foot to the post office on my own. I was kicking pebbles and picking up little multicoloured stones as I walked along the road.

When I arrived at the post office, the postmistress gave me a few letters rubber-banded together to give to my mother. Being curious, I looked at the outside of the envelopes, checking to see if there were any airmail envelopes, as we called them back in those days. This denoted a letter from abroad. It was always a special moment for me when I received a letter from my sister Ve, who had migrated to Canada.

The Post Office

I saw no airmail letters in the pile. But I did notice that one of the letters was from Titchfield High School, addressed to Joyce and Kenneth Wilson,

Durham Gap District, Portland. At the time, this did not ring any bells. I was not happy because there were no letters from Ve, as I had expected.

I took the letters to my mother. She opened the letter from Titchfield High School, and I could see the smile on Mama's face. She looked at me in astonishment as she informed me that I was being offered a place there. She said the school had requested for us to attend a meeting for orientation at the school the following week, on Monday at nine in the morning. Included in the letter was the pattern of the school uniform, including the strange-looking physical-education uniform pattern, and a book list.

My mama and I were both happy about this great news, yet in our excitement, we could not help discussing whether this was some sort of error. We read the letter over and over to make sense of the content as we started accepting there was only one *Marie Wilson* and one *Joyce Wilson* in our small community. My mother and I went shopping to purchase school materials at the last minute. My mother made my uniforms herself, including the physical-education uniforms, and my books were purchased at Sangster's Bookstore.

CHAPTER 10

HIGH SCHOOL

My high school life started on a bright Monday morning in September in the late 1970s. My mother made my uniform waist bigger than my size deliberately so there was a little gap at the back. This made me to feel uncomfortable, as my white uniform blouse would rise above my waist, prompting me to keep pulling down the blouse through an opening my mother made in the pocket for this purpose. According to my mother, she made the uniform waist big because I was growing, so that the uniform would last for a longer time.

My first day, it was difficult adjusting to the new learning environment. I was placed in class "one south." This was a semi-open-space classroom structured towards the back of the school, bordered with decorated blocks to one side. It was bordered on the other side by a narrow area of land overlooking the sea, which was called the *battery*. I could hear the splashing of sea waves as they battered against the stony banks that formed a barrier at the back of the school compound.

High school had its challenges. Within the first couple of weeks, I made new friends, or thought I did. It was hard thinking of someone as a friend who did not think the same as I did.

Initially, at the start of secondary education, I lived with my older sister Carol. I was 11, and she treated me like a grown-up. She gave me her two small children to care for and all her household chores, including the washing, cooking, and ironing—not just for her children, but also for herself and her partner. I hand-washed bed linen and clothes as well.

I was told that I was not going to come out to anything. Even though I did all the housework as dictated by my sister, nothing I did ever pleased her. The more I worked, the more work she gave me to do. If my sister was cooking, she would ask me to clean up before, in between, and after cooking. She made me collect all the ingredients that she needed for cooking, such as spring onions, thyme, onions, scotch bonnet pepper, and garlic. I had to prep and have everything ready for her.

My brother Geoffery and I, who also lived there, once planned a hunger strike for three days, deliberately missing meals. This did not change anything. It went unnoticed.

I had to take responsibility for my development and for how I chose to think and feel about myself if I was going to take control my life. I kept to the notion that if it were within my power to do so, I would prove others wrong when they shared or acted out their thoughts that I would never achieve success in life. This was easier said than done, as avoiding contact and trying to do things as an entity made it more challenging. Although achieving in one aspect, I was losing out on other important life components.

This can be supported by a math teacher, Ms Willi, who once told me in front of a class of students, "Don't get swell-headed." This was after I had scored an A in an exam. I was in the process of assisting a student who had repeated the class, as she was struggling with her calculations. As a result of the embarrassment from the teacher, I developed an intense dislike for her as well as the subject. I deliberately missed all her mathematics classes.

Instead of going to mathematics class, I would go to the home-economics centre to cook and bake. This was where I met Miss Spence-Brown, the home economics teacher who taught me how to make my first cake. Missing class was not a problem to me, as I knew that my parents would never find out. They did not check my work or show any interest in my grades. Although I learnt to cook and bake, I lost out on learning a key subject, mathematics, which caused some setbacks in my academic life. I could not get myself to accept the ridicule from my mathematics teacher.

What I did not understand at the time was that my mathematics teacher already had her knowledge, and that in the end, I was the one who was going to be losing out, not her. Contrary to this experience in high school, there were other teachers who sought to help in my development and acknowledge the most minute accomplishment.

As I progressed through Mr Harris's geography class, he took every opportunity to expose hidden characteristics I never knew I had. I still have memories of some of the geography lecture discussions, especially one of his teaching sessions about hurricanes. His expressions were astounding, and the way he put his lesson across kept me focused throughout the session. I can still recall some his teaching sessions as if it were yesterday.

Whenever the hurricane season comes around, I always remember that he taught me this: "Hurricanes often develop from easterly waves, which are low-pressure masses of air that enter the Caribbean during the months of May to November. They appear on an average every five days and may cause rain." I often share this information with students and use this reference as a tool in my teaching and learning strategies.

Building my confidence was a crucial characteristic in my learning and development.

According to Marcus Garvey, "If you haven't confidence in self you are twice defeated in the race of life. With confidence you have won even before you have started."

CHAPTER 11

MEETING MY SOULMATE

THEN

NOW

On Saturdays, I would go to the Seventh-day Adventist Church. This was a spiritual and social activity that I looked forward to. It was at this church that I met Euthan when I was about 12 years old. Initially, we were just friends, and it remained so as we progressed through high school up to fourth form.

One Wednesday evening, my mother asked me to take some food for my sister in-law who was hospitalized. I dropped the food off at the maternity unit at Port Antonio Hospital. I was walking back home along the coastline when I met Euthan along the way. He agreed to follow me home, as it was beginning to get dark, and the road to my home was a bit lonely.

As we were walking along, my neighbour drove past us and blew his horn. In virtue, I did not give any thought to this. We were nearing the slip road to the house where I lived when I saw my mother in the distance walking briskly in my direction. As she came closer, I noticed that she had a guava-tree branch in her hand. Euthan walked away as she approached us.

Being too obedient and too disciplined, I walked up to my mother when she called me, even though I could see the rage in her eyes. She grabbed me by my clothes, and in the interim, my skirt got torn off. The guava branch was a whip for me. There was no explanation throughout this difficult and embarrassing encounter, and I had no clue what I had done to deserve this.

Eventually, after many hours had passed and I refused to stop crying, she said the neighbour told her that he drove past me and did not stop to give me a lift as he saw me walking home with a policeman's son.

The next time I saw Euthan, he said, "Now that your mother beat you like that, I know that you will not talk to me anymore."

I told Euthan, "I am not going to take that beating for nothing. I was not thinking about our friendship that way, but I am interested now." This was when our real meet-up started.

His uncle Terley, who was an engineer living and working in the United States, was on holiday in Jamaica. I met Terley at Euthan's parents' home.

He seemed intrigued to meet me. He asked Euthan's mother, "Icy, who is this young lady?"

Euthan's mother replied, "Ask Euthan."

Terley said to Euthan, "Boy, you really have taste."

Terley was supportive toward us throughout our relationship. He even bought my wedding ring.

Euthan asked my parents' permission to marry me when I was in my late teens. My mother told me, "Euthan spoke to us. He told us, 'Marie is not my mother's choice. Marie is not my father's choice. Marie is *my* choice.'" The difficult encounter with my mother as well as knowing that I was Euthan's choice was what helped me make the decision to say *yes* to his proposal. The friendship blossomed into a matrimonial relationship a couple of years after we finished high school.

Today, we are still married. I love him, I hate him, but I cannot do without him. I have been through too much to leave him. The reality of life never made our experiences the same. Each of us had our own scenarios.

CHAPTER 12

THE NIGHT I SLEPT IN THE CHURCH

Back to the early start of my high-school life, when I was living with my sister Carol. After some months, she relocated from Portland to live in Kingston, Jamaica. Following this, my mother found an accommodation for me to live with a Christian woman called Mrs B.

The accommodation was located next to a cemetery. I was fearful looking at the graves, especially at night. I told my father that I was scared to live by the cemetery, as all I could see was the vast expanse of graves. He said, "Be afraid of the living. The dead will never hurt you."

I was apprehensive about staying at the boarded accommodation too, yet I had no choice. The decision was already made. As a child, I had to do as I was told by my parents. I dared not ask too many questions about the decisions they made either.

Life was not what I had expected. In my new home, we had family worship regularly. This helped me in many ways. The Bible verses and the prayers helped me face daily challenges, and the positive comments from Mrs B were always reassuring. Mrs B often told me that I should not worry; I would achieve what I wanted to achieve in life. She often referred to a list of individuals whom she claimed passed through her hands and were doing well in the pastoral field. One served as the president of an international conference of churches. These reassuring comments gave me great hope, although I had no intent to be a pastor.

As usual, on Tuesdays I went with Mrs B to choir practice at the Seventh-Day Adventist Church on Sommer's Town Road, Port Antonio. I was tired after a long school day, and it was a two-mile walk from school to home and back to the church. I could barely keep my eyes open, so I went down the aisle of the church and went to sleep on one of the long wooden benches near the side-exit door. I hoped that Mrs B would see me when the practice was done even if I was asleep. But she finished her practice and went home, leaving me behind sleeping in the church.

In the wee hours of the night during my sleep, I felt as though someone was standing over me. As I opened my eyes, I was staring in the face of a man. My initial thought was, *Is it a ghost?* I was speechless. I tried to scream, but I was frozen, and no words came out of my mouth.

The man I thought to be a ghost turned out to be the church watchman. He reassured me not to be so frightened, as no harm would come to me. He repeatedly identified himself as "Brother Walker." I was still dazed and thought I was in a dream. Through the dim light, I saw empty wooden benches all around. I was wondering where I was, and was this all real?

Mr Walker pointed to the big wall clock and asked me, "What are you doing here?"

As I got my thoughts together, I replied, "I came to choir practice with Mrs B."

He said, "The choir practice finished a long time ago. Everyone went home."

I asked, "Where is Mrs B?"

He said, "She went home."

I looked up at the platform where the choir practice had been held. It was empty, and the place was in silence. I was anxious to the point that I could hardly breathe. This must have been a panic attack.

Mr Walker pointed to the paint pan and brush in his hand. He explained that he had come in early to do maintenance work in the church. Mixed feelings played on my mind, as my thoughts wandered to the valley and then to the mountain. The caretaker for the church had come to do his work in the early hours of the morning. He said that he saw the unfamiliar figure curled up on the bench while he was preparing to start painting, so he had come to see what it was.

From my recollections of the incident, this could have been a totally different scenario. I was kept safe through it all, which took me back to the guardian angels I heard my mother pray about as well as helping to build my own faith.

Mr Walker agreed to accompany me home. We walked the dark lonely road adjacent to the coastline. It was quiet and peaceful, with only the sound of the gentle sea waves battering to and from the shore. We turned off the main road onto the left side road, which was referred to by residents as Cemetery Lane. I kept my eyes fixed on the road; apart from Mr Walker, there was not a living soul in sight. All was still except for the on-and-off chirping sounds of crickets.

As we arrived at the door to the house where I lived, Mr Walker knocked on the door. We waited a while for a response, then Mrs B came to the door with an angry temper flaring.

"Where have you been?" she shouted. I am sure that I was much angrier than her. Yet she muttered again in a husky voice, with her false teeth shaking and falling out, "Where have you been?"

It took me a while before I could talk. I was just thinking, *How dare Mrs B go home and leave me in the church sleeping.* She may have been worried that I had eloped, but to me, I felt let down by the very person who should have been caring for me.

I tried to explain, but my explanation was to no avail. Mrs B was too busy sharing her own thoughts as to what she perceived had happened. She told me how disappointed she was that I left the church and went about my own business. She said, "You are rude. When choir practice finished, I did not see you. I thought you had gone off with someone."

Mr Walker told her he went to the church early to carry out his work and found me sleeping on the bench. She did not appear to even be listening or making any effort to show understanding of what he was saying. She continued to say I was nowhere to be seen.

I do not know if she ever believed my story. Although she eventually calmed down, she did not show any remorse. I went to my room and whispered to myself, "I will not be in this house much longer." If my guardian thought that I was missing, what action did she take to find me?

Sometimes my meal was thick porridge or a fried egg with cold breadfruit. This reminded me of the boiled breadfruit that my father fed to his animals. Miss B had to work, and oftentimes I was left with her incapable husband, who himself was physically challenged and struggled with simple cooking chores. Each time it was mealtime, I thought of the food that was wasted in my home every day.

I do not believe for one minute that these people meant bad. I just think they seemed to do what was easiest for them. My father was generous with food, and there was always more than enough to eat. My father prepared up to three large chickens at a time. My mother was a little mean, so my father would tell us children to eat some of the chicken before my mother got home from work, so that she would not know how many chickens he had cooked.

He would sell a goat or cow to the butchers and would end up buying back half of the meat. All this I had taken for granted was now wishful thinking, as I now knew what it was to be hungry. When I visited my parents with my brother Geoffery for the weekend, my father always gave us boxes of food to take back with us. This included yellow yams, sweet potatoes, bananas, plantains, and fruits and vegetables that were in season.

Sunday evenings, I would walk with my brother Geoffery to the bus stop with our food. Sometimes I would stop by my grandmother and give my bag of food to her, since I thought she needed it and the bag was too heavy to carry. My brother took his box of food as far as the bridge of the Rio Grande River in Portland, and then he dropped his box of food in the river.

My brother was an overly proud young man. When I asked why he threw the food in the river, he told me that he did not want any of his friends to see him carrying the box of food on his head. These priceless ground provisions and fruits all washed down the river as they were taken away by torrents of water.

There were fruit trees of all description on the farm. Our father had sumptuous amounts of fruits daily. To name some, there were jackfruit, grapefruit, tangerine, orange, guinep, plums, tamarind, guava, orange, star apple, custard apple, soursop, pear, lemon, limes, coolie plum, rose apple, and pineapple, not to mention the very tasty turpentine and the big sid mango, which were my favourite.

My mother, being too stern, seemed to take great pleasure in meting out disciplinary measures for everything, anything, and nothing. Her comment after would be, "Why are you crying?" or "Stop the crying!" or "You want something to cry for?" As children, we had to stand straight with feet together when talking to adults. You dare not lean or put your hands on your sides (akimbo) when talking to my mother.

As siblings, we could not use some words in conversation with our mother, such as *what, how,* and *then.* Mama considered these words to be disrespectful when used by a child during a conversation with adults. My sisters Janel and Michelle were either forgetting not to use these words or they probably just liked pressing the wrong buttons. Especially Michelle. In her usual responses, she would say, "Then mama, why mama," and so on. So they were the main siblings who had to go through disciplinary actions.

Nowadays, I'm amazed at the things children get away with, even my own children. Society has placed a lot of restrictions on what parents can and cannot do. But this was the way of life in my childhood. My mother was even keen to read my letters as a teenager, just to find out what I was getting up to and if there was a need to intervene. Once, she found a letter written to me by my husband (then fiancé), and although my father saved me from the physical punishment, I was given stern warnings.

CHAPTER 13

THE SPANISH TEST

My first Spanish test took place in a classroom adjacent to the school auditorium. I had just walked into class and, as usual, I took my pen from my bag and put my bag under the desk. One of the students, Jan (not her real name), told the teacher I was copying. I had no idea we were even getting a test, and I had not even received the question paper. I had no clue what the test was about.

I tried to explain to the teacher that I was only getting my pen and I did not have my test paper yet. She did not listen when I tried to explain this. As I tried to speak, she kept on talking, so

I could not get a word in. She repeatedly said, "Don't even start. You are getting a zero." I was confused by Jan's comment, but I was even more confused by the teacher's response. She was a new foreign teacher, and she did not work for long at the school.

I confronted Jan during break time to find out the reasoning behind her actions. She told me that she was sorry for doing this. She mentioned that the teacher also knew that I had only just walked into the class. I was never given a chance to prove my innocence. I lost interest in the subject I had wanted to learn so badly, and I eventually out of shame gave up learning Spanish.

Both Jan and the teacher left the school shortly after the incident. My only regret is that I never had the opportunity to explain myself to that teacher. I experienced similar false accusations in my work life too. These incidents often have a negative impact, as they did for me, especially in terms of trust issues, confidence-building, and maintaining confidence.

CHAPTER 14

THE TEACHER VS. THE GUARDIAN

After I graduated from high school, my parents decided to board me out again to attend college. This time it was in Kingston, the capital of Jamaica. I moved to live in a beautiful sophisticated residential area of Kingston. There was an upscale shopping centre, Manor Park, about five minutes' walk from the house where I lived. I visited the food hall on a regular basis to get delicious ice cream and other goodies.

My first term at this college was excellent. The teacher showed expertise in his field. He knew the textbook from cover to cover. Yet he never used a textbook when teaching.

Months went by, and my first year of college finally ended. As I moved up from level one to level two, the challenges with the new teacher increased. There were students who would change each other's seats around, and this could sometimes be a little disruptive during class.

The accounts teacher, Mr C, often called out my name even though I was not the one disrupting his class. Sometimes it made me wonder if having a good attitude and being respectful really worked for everyone. I started questioning to find out what the problem was. Mr C not only asked me to change my seat several times in the class while other students giggled, but he also threatened to cancel my accounts exam, for which I had already paid.

Mr C informed me a couple of months before the exam that I would not be doing the accounts level two exam, as he was going to sell my exam to another student. This student was my friend Lilly, who did not even put in an application or show any interest in doing the exam. Lilly was a respectful student, a loyal friend and classmate.

As the examination time was getting closer, my guardian Aunt Bell asked me, "Why are you not studying for the exam?" I told her that my teacher sold my place, and I was waiting for a refund. Therefore, there was no point studying.

She asked why. I told Aunt Bell that, according to Mr C, I was not going to pass the accounts exam, so he made the decision to sell my exam to a student he believed would pass it.

Aunt Bell was not happy about this. She was furious. She said, "What are you telling me? I did accounts. I have seen your work. Yes, you will do your exam, and yes, you will pass."

I gave Aunt Bell the contact number for the college and the name of the principal as she requested. I overheard her on the phone telling the principal, "I know Marie. She is capable; she is going to sit her exam and she is going to pass. You mean you don't know about this? So who authorize this action?"

Listening to this conversation made me realize that Aunt Bell believed in my ability to pass this exam. This made me want to live up to her expectation—even though at this point, I had doubts regarding my abilities, as the encounter with Mr C really knocked my self-confidence.

The following day, I was in class when the principal for the college, Ms T, called me to her office. She stated that my aunt had contacted the college. I told her that I would like to do my exam, as Aunt Bell had suggested. By this time, my friend Lilly had informed me that she would not be purchasing my exam place, as instigated by Mr C, as she was migrating to North America to join her mother.

Mrs Moore, my English teacher, met up with me to find out why I was not sitting my accounts examination. With tears welling up, I explained the situation. Mrs Moore said that she would speak to the principal and the accounts teacher, Mr C, on my behalf.

She said, "You have a good command of the English language, so you can master any subject. English is the fundamental subject for learning any other subject. Never let anyone tell you otherwise."

Though I did not understand her statement clearly regarding command of the English language, I was grateful for the reassurance and support. But I felt that Mr C had already made his decision. My initial thought was, *How can English help someone to pass accounts, which is another subject?* For every area of study, both in college and university, I reflected on those words from my English teacher.

The interventions from Aunt Bell and my English teacher, Mrs Moore, were auspicious. As a result of their support, I could now do my exam, despite Mr C's insistent effort for me not to do so.

It was a Monday morning in the 1980s. I left home with butterflies in my stomach as I travelled to Piccadilly Road and then to the Overseas Examination Centre in Kingston, Jamaica. I looked for my examination ID number and took my seat in the front row. Towards the start of exam, I saw the accounts teacher, Mr C, walking in. He stood at the front of the room opposite to where I was sitting with a mild smirk on his face.

This was what I had dreaded most. Just seeing that teacher made me very anxious. It was surprising to see him there, as this was an external exam. I even had difficulty holding the pen to write, as my hands were shaky and dripping with sweat.

My legs were shaking under the desk too as I gently patted my hands, on my clothes to dry the sweat. Other students were busy writing away as the examiner read the rules and asked us to begin.

For the first hour, I wrote nothing, as I could not get my thoughts together even to start. I began to pray for guidance, knowledge, memory, and strength. I picked up my pen as I remembered Aunt Bell's words to me: "You are going to pass."

As I turned the page, I quickly read the instructions and tried to decide which questions to tackle first, as time was running out. I skipped through the questions. There was an income and expenditure account question on the paper. Having looked at income and expenditure the night before the exam, I thought I must do this question. There were a couple more selections, but I did what I knew best first, which was the income and expenditure question.

I had tried to discuss this topic with my soulmate Euthan (who was my best friend then) the night before the exam but he was not interested in the topic and said, "That is not coming." I was happy I'd followed my gut feeling to read over this topic.

I looked over to where Euthan was sitting in the far corner to my right, and he did not look up, as he was busy writing. We were both doing similar business studies, and although we were not in the same college, we sat the same external exam. I worked through the questions one at a time as quickly as I could until the time was up.

After the exam, everyone was talking about the paper. I met up with Euthan to find out which questions he did. I shared my ordeal with him, of how nerves got the better of me when I saw my teacher in the exam room. I also asked him how he handled the income and expenditure account question. He replied, "I didn't do it."

After the exam, weeks and months passed. One Monday morning, as soon as I walked into my classroom, a classmate told me to go to the office to see the principal. I asked, "What is the story again?" Usually when one was called by the principal, the news was not good, so my first thought was, *What have I done?*

I was dismayed when I arrived in the office and saw other students laughing and discussing the exam results, as displayed on the notice board. I looked at the board and at the top of the exam result list was my name, Marie Wilson. I doubted myself so much that I checked the spelling again, asking other students if this was the list for those who had passed the accounts exam or those who had failed.

I was now shrieking with excitement, as this was indeed the pass list. It was a rewarding feeling with my promotion to the accounts stage three class that morning—the advanced accounts class.

As I entered the classroom, I met the teacher, Mr C. He looked at me and said, "Wonders never cease." I could have said the same about him, as I knew he was not expecting me to pass.

I reflected on my primary-school experience and decided I would prove my teachers wrong, especially those who taught me and did not expect success from me. It was a good lesson not to be put off by so-called friends, teachers, and others who do not have your best interest at heart. As talk show host and author Oprah Winfrey once said, "If you surround yourself with negative people, they will drain your energy."

This teacher's attitude towards me had a significant impact on my emotional well-being as well as my learning. Each time I went through an embarrassing, belittling situation, it cast a doubt on my abilities. I felt like I was a failure. I was giving in to his expectations of me, which further pushed me into passivity. Without quick input from Aunt Bell, the outcome could have been different. I would not have even questioned the teacher's actions for fear of failure and embarrassment.

After all that push from Mr Christian to get me where I was, another math teacher at a prominent college told me that I was wasting the government's money and that the baby could do better than me.

As a teenager, a police officer assaulted me and tried to put me in jail. He pulled me by my clothes from the streets of Port Antonio Town and took me to the police station. He demanded for me to go in a grilled cage. This incident happened after he made an overly friendly gesture to which I did not agree. His friend who was present at the time said to him, "Box her. She deserves a box." A few years later I nursed the same police officer on an in-patient ward. This taught me many lessons.

CHAPTER 15

MISSED DROWNING

I was travelling from Kingston to Portland, Jamaica, on a weekend trip with my friend Billy when it started raining. The Rio Grande had flooded, and the water had come up over the bridge. We stopped to assess the situation.

We were approached by a group of boys who told us that it was OK to drive through the water. In the middle of the bridge, the car engine shut off. The car was submerged in water. The boys came to give us a push. By this time, the water was up to our waist. I placed the children to stand on the seats, as the water was rising fast.

Then along came a truck from a side road. Someone on the truck threw us a rope, and one of the boys helped us tie the rope to the car. As we drove off, feeling happy that we were out of the water, the rope burst, and the car came to a stop on the brow of the hill leading to Snow Hill Village, Portland. This was indeed a danger. If the car started running back, we would be heading for the river that had already flooded its banks.

Billy first prayed, and then he asked me to pray. I replied, "I can't. God is going to think I am too presumptuous because I don't want to die." I said, "Let the children pray. God will listen to them. They are innocent, and their prayer is genuine."

Billy insisted that I pray, and I was left with no choice. I thought, *We are going to all drown if the car runs back in the river.* Time was short, as this was happening fast.

I closed my eyes to ask favour from God. I prayed for guidance, wisdom, understanding, and protection. Billy tried one last time to start the car, and to our surprise, the car started. As we drove to the top of the hill at the Stony Hill T-junction, the car shut off. No matter what Billy did, the car would not restart.

It was now dark and getting late. We had to call it a night to remember. We started walking until we got to Passley Gardens Teachers College, where we spent the night with my incredibly good friend Mrs Bernard, who warmly received us. We were happy to make up temporary beds just to be safe for the night.

> *There can be only one judge, the eternally self-existent one. When in his awful majesty he sits surrounded by myriads angel witnesses with their unerring testimony, then the pompous word of men will count for nothing.— Ernest Marter, "Daniel and the Revelation"*

CHAPTER 16

STARTING WORK

After leaving college, I attended the Stony Hill Heart Academy in St. Andrew, Jamaica. It was as if I was going backwards to go forward, and sometimes this was necessary for me in the given circumstances. This college was easily accessible, and I did not have the money to pursue the course I wanted to do in university at the time. My parents having paid my college fees, I did not want to ask them for any more financial support, as by then I had chosen to take on adulthood and had moved out on my own into rented accommodation.

I finished the one-year training and started my working experience at the National Insurance

Office, Ministry of Works and Pensions. Following my placement, I was offered a position as a clerical officer. I worked in the Ministry of National Insurance whilst waiting for my exam results in commerce and economics. I later changed jobs and started working for the Ministry of Education. Sometimes my challenges were good, as they certainly took me out of my comfort zone.

One morning, I dropped off my two young children at school and rushed to work almost breathless by the time I got to the top of the stairs, only to be approached by my supervisor, who asked, "Miss Newman, what happened to you this morning?" It was not so much what she said, it was how she said it.

I replied, "Nothing."

She then stated, "So when the personnel officer asks me, is that what I should tell her?"

I replied, "Yes."

It was the way she asked, it was the way I responded. I decided I could do better than this, and so I decided to leave the job without clearly thinking it through. I learned for the future that I must be cautious how I manage my frustrations.

A schoolmate from high school was working in another department and tried to encourage me to stay, but it was too late. I had already handed in my notice. She said, "No good person would encourage you to leave your job without first having another job." She enquired how I would manage financially. At this point, it did not matter to me. All I wanted was support at work, for the job.

I worked briefly in another department, always striving to complete my daily targets and working above expectations. I did not expect compliments or praise, but my supervisor started asking me to do things outside of my work duties, and I was beginning to feel obligated and not appreciated or valued, so this was the wide awakening that it was time for me to move on.

I started planning my leaving party even before I handed in my resignation. The following morning, on my way to work, I stopped at Kingston School of Nursing, Jamaica, to get an application pack. Once I filled in the application form, I knew that was the end of my job. I was now one step closer to becoming a nurse.

I met with my work colleagues for the party and bid good-bye to the job. I visited my past high school to get a reference from the principal, who told me that he had to check my file before writing the reference. On his return, he said, "This reference is not going to be hard. Guess what? At the start of school, you put on your form that your ambition was to become a nurse. In fourth form, you were placed in 4 Engineering

Science because you showed competence in doing the sciences, plus you have a clean slate."

I felt happy with this comment, even though I could not recall writing that my ambition was to become a nurse. Whilst in college, I was thinking of becoming a chartered accountant.

CHAPTER 17

THE LOST AND FOUND MOTHER AND DAUGHTER

I lost contact with Aunt Una for a long time. I had no phone number or contact address for her. I began searching different databases from family to online resources. At the point of giving up, I made a final attempt using her husband's surname.

Finally, in 1982, I made contact via a US telephone service, and she answered the call. I overcame failed efforts by continuous trying. I put all my commitment into finding her, and it paid off in the end.

My aunt sounded excited over the phone and seemed pleased to hear from me again. She called me "my lost and found daughter," and I called her "my found mother." We agreed never to lose touch with each other again.

Life with my Aunt Una was great. She was my mother who did not give birth to me. I could not have asked for more, and it seemed the time was just about right when we reunited.

I went to America to spend quality time with my found mother. The mother-daughter relationship was superb. When my aunt found out that I was expecting a baby, I thought she was going to be upset. Instead, she was overly excited for me.

During my pregnancy, I had a lot of cravings, the main one being for grapes and red apples. My aunt would buy me an entire box of grapes. All I had to do was mentioned that I wanted something, and she would go out of her way to make sure I would get it.

In 1996, my daughter was born at New Rochelle Hospital in New York. I was in excruciating labour pain from the contractions, and the pain was becoming more unbearable. Aunt Una was in the process of going to visit her brother in Canada for the weekend. She fried fish and baked me my favourite orange cake before going on her trip. She told me how disappointed she was that I would not be going with her to Canada.

I hid my pain and waited for her to leave. As she drove off in her Toyota Previa, I watched her speed away. As soon as the car was out of sight, I quickly called my sister Michelle to take me to the hospital, as the pain was now worse than before, and the contractions were quicker and becoming unbearable.

My sister asked me, "What am I going to drive?"

I replied, "Anything."

She said, "Dennis [her husband] is at work, and he has the car."

I looked out the window into the driveway and saw that Uncle Cecil's car was still parked there. I told Michelle to come now, as we could borrow Cecil's car or take a taxi. I tried calling a taxi, but it was taking forever; none was available within the time frame I needed.

Michelle came within ten minutes, but it seemed like ten hours. We drove Uncle Cecil's car to New Rochelle. Within less than ten minutes of arriving at the hospital, Baby Xeena was born. It was quick thinking to leave at the time we did, as had I delayed much longer, the baby would have been born at home, or in the car.

On arrival at the hospital, I was rushed to the labour ward. I was examined by the doctor and informed that I was ten centimetres dilated and ready for delivery. I gave birth to a bouncing baby girl.

Aunt Una spent the weekend in Canada with her brother. When she returned to New York, I was home with the baby. The baby's name, Xeena, came from the warrior princess. Although Aunt Una was happy to see us, she was annoyed that she was not present for the birth of the baby. She said that she would have postponed her trip to Canada if she had known the baby was going to come so early.

We joked and laughed about the situation, about being good at not showing I was in pain. I did not want her to have to cancel her planned trip to visit her brother.

I was well supported during the postnatal period. Aunt Una would lie in bed with the baby on her chest so that I could get some rest. She would be talking to the baby as if she understood what Xeena was saying. My aunt would be saying things like, "Xeena, you are so intelligent; you are listening to my heartbeat, which is good, as it is keeping you quiet for your mother to get some rest. You are an American. You are unique; soon you will be eating collard greens, pancakes, and waffles."

I laughed at what my aunt was telling the newborn baby. I asked my aunt what she meant by collard greens. I knew my aunt meant well, even if things did not sound right to me.

This early nurturing seemed to instil some traits in Xeena that I observed later in life. One example: When Xeena left high school, she went to college to do a diploma baccalaureate. After a few months, I called her teacher to get an update on her progress. The teacher told me, "Xeena is the worst person in my class. She is bright, but she does not want to do the work anymore." There was no explanation for this when I asked the teacher.

When I asked Xeena what was going on, she said, "Mother, you will never believe the reasoning behind this, as everything my teacher tells you about me is gospel for you."

With all that I had been through, I had learned to listen more, so I asked Xeena what she wanted to do. She said, "Mother, as I have told Dad, I want to study acting."

In my mind, I was thinking, *Where would this acting take Xeena?, more so as a black girl.* Given the feedback from her teacher, though, I thought I must do something, so I applied to a college on her behalf. Xeena was invited for an interview, and I was allowed to accompany her.

At the interview, Xeena was asked by one of the panel members, "Why did you apply to do this particular course?" Another panel member mentioned that "only about one in ten thousand persons who study acting may get a part in a movie, if that much."

Xeena responded, "I don't want to spend the next five years of my life studying what my parents want me to do."

The next question asked was, "We noticed that you also applied to study business. What is the reason behind this?"

Xeena said, "If I don't get a part in a movie, I can open my own business."

The response from the lead interviewer was, "I love that. You can start tomorrow morning at nine." The interview concluded here.

Xeena was offered a place to do acting and business studies. On completion of college, she went on to a prominent university to further her study in acting. I tried to persuade her to do something different, but in the end, she stuck to her decision.

I told Xeena, "Since this is your choice, do not come back home with less than a grade one."

On graduation, Xeena was awarded a 1:1 for her BSc. I was lying in bed when Xeena knocked on my door. I invited her in. Xeena brought me her result and said, "Mother, here is your one."

Xeena has already managed to secure parts in plays and advertisements, and she is currently on her journey to becoming the actress she wants to be. I hope this will help others to make those small goals and grow to be what they want to be. Time waits on no one. The best time to do anything is always now.

CHAPTER 18

TRAGEDY

I had the most special relationship with my Aunt Una; it was a special feeling to know I had a genuine someone to listen to me and help me come up with options and solutions when the going was tough. She made the most challenging situations looked easy. Her usual comment was, "Don't worry alone. We are in this together."

We had that special connection, and I have yet to find another person with such characteristics. I know what it is to set goals for tomorrow that never happen, not to mention the regret of losing the opportunity of doing what I could have done yesterday.

My aunt Una and I had planned a holiday to visit Jamaica after the birth of Xeena, with the intention to tour all fourteen parishes. In the midst of our travelling around the island, things began to change drastically.

The problems started with the insensitive immigration officer at the airport. We were kept for a long time in the immigration hall. My aunt was getting frustrated as the officer searched through our luggage. He took out our belongings and then asked us to repack them. We were exhausted by the time he gave us the clearance to leave. No empathy was shown towards a three-month-old baby and my aunt's foster children, who were all tired and restless after the long flight. It was a relief to get out of the airport.

When we arrived at our destination, we unpacked our bags. Aunt Una did the cooking as usual. We ate and settled into bed for the night. Everything seemed to be falling into place as was previously planned.

Our first couple of days in Jamaica went well. We went to church on the Saturday. During the night, my aunt was dancing to the music as my husband played his drum set. We all joined in the dance.

The following day, we went to Portland to drop off a barrel of goods Aunt Una had brought for her brother-in-law at Durham Gap. My aunt's sister had died during the planning phase of our trip; however, she wanted her brother-in-law to have the things she had purchased for them. When she stopped to give her brother-in-law his barrel, he did not seem surprised, as we had anticipated, that my aunt was back in Jamaica shortly after having attended her sister's funeral a few weeks prior.

When my aunt had returned to New York after the funeral, she'd reported feeling unwell. She went to see her doctor, who told her she'd picked up a bug in Jamaica. My aunt told me that she'd only eaten food from two people in Jamaica. She was puzzled as to how she could have picked up a bug.

Still, she took her medication and some ginger tea. After completing her prescribed course of antibiotic treatment, my aunt said that she felt much better. The symptoms subsided, except for on-and-off heartburn, which she complained of. She was taking Maalox, which she said helped with the heartburn. She had brought a bottle of this with her on our trip to Jamaica.

During our vacation, my aunt suggested that we should take a road trip from Kingston to Portland via St Thomas on our way back to Kingston. We left Kingston early on the Sunday morning, hoping to get into St Thomas by mid-morning. We watched the breaking of dawn and the rising of the sun, and all seemed bright and beautiful.

Whilst we were driving closer towards Bath Fountain, St Thomas, the weather suddenly changed. The bright sky was now looking dark and gloomy, overshadowed with a dull glow. The atmosphere was quiet. I asked my husband if we were in the right place as we stopped at Bath Fountain, a known tourist area. It was our first destination in St Thomas.

I decided to stay in the car. I had an early premonition that something was not right with the environment. It looked dull and overcast, as if it was going to rain. I kept looking around, as visitors to the island sometimes can easily be targeted.

I watched a couple of boys walk by. Contrary to my thoughts, the boys were probably just going about their own business, looking for customers for body massage to earn some money. My aunt kept asking me to come out of the car. I did for a little while, but I did not feel like going into the water. My aunt returned to the car. No one seemed enthusiastic about staying, so we decided to leave and come back another day when the weather was better.

It started drizzling; the sky was still overcast. As we drove down the hilly slope towards the main road, we saw people selling beautiful breadfruit and mangos. Aunt Una asked if I was going to get some. I told her that when we got to the main road, we would get some of the fruit. In my mind, I was thinking that we were easy targets if robbers pounced on us, as the road was so deserted.

As we drove about another two minutes, my aunt said, "I am not feeling well." I looked at her and saw a sudden drop on her face. I tried to feel her pulse; it was weak and thready. Her skin was sweaty, clammy, and cold.

I told my daughter Seon to put a comforter under Aunt Una's head. Seon shouted back, "Mom, she feels cold, like dead." I thought, *what is this young child saying?*

I asked my husband to stop the car so Aunt Una could get some fresh air. On a quick assessment of the situation. I knew something was wrong. I told Euthan to drive to the nearest hospital. I was relieved when we reached it because my thoughts were that as long as I could get her to the hospital quickly, the doctor would be able to help.

On arriving at the hospital, I was greeted by one of my batch mates. She was the nurse working in the accident and emergency department, so I thought, *oh, my aunt is in good hands.*

I asked the nurse if the doctor knew what he was doing, and she said, "Oh yes, he is a very good doctor."

I left my aunt for a few minutes in what I thought were capable medical hands. I headed back to the car to breastfeed my three-month-old baby and then quickly rushed back in the hospital. The doctor told me he had given my aunt nitroglycerine, magnesium trisilicate, and Valium. She was still looking unwell, so we drove to Kingston Public Hospital (KPH), the major hospital on the island.

On arrival at this hospital, my aunt said, "I feel as if I am having a stroke or a heart attack." She never made it, despite all the efforts of the nurses and doctors at KPH. The nurse in charge, Joanna, came over to check her blood pressure and looked at her eyelids. The nurse mentioned how pale she looked and asked me to go and register her, which I did. Throughout all of this, I was still thinking, *she will be in hospital only for a short time. I will ensure she gets the best care.* I was thinking how we both would soon be laughing about the whole scenario, but the tragedy of life had different plans.

I went to check on the baby again and asked my husband to stay with my aunt. Within minutes, I saw my husband running towards me, almost breathless. He said, "Let's pray."

I asked, "What happened?"

He said, "I heard a doctor say, 'She stopped breathing.'"

I asked loudly, "What do you mean? Is she dead?"

He said, "No, I don't think so. The doctors are looking after her."

I do not remember what I did with my baby, but I started running. I rushed past the nurses in the accident and emergency room and made my way to the resuscitation room. I saw doctors trying frantically to resuscitate my aunt. The doctors were signalling for me to leave the room. I just stood there, frozen. I wanted to see what was happening and how I could help. This was my most helpless moment.

I watched as she took her last loud breath. In my panic-stricken state, I asked the accident and emergency sister, "What do you think?"

She replied, "She is a goner."

The doctors kept trying to resuscitate her. One of them administered adrenaline. As a nurse, this was the situation in which I felt the most helpless. I wanted to do so much, but there was nothing I could do. It was out of my hands.

I was praying, "Dear God, save her, save her, please, do not let her die." I heard loud groaning sounds coming from my aunt. At first, I thought, *oh, she is still alive, she is coming around.* I later understood that these were abnormal breath sounds.

She never made it. The result of the autopsy was haemorrhagic pancreatitis. At the post-mortem, the doctor asked me, "What did she have to eat or drink?" I could only tell her what I knew she ate.

As my aunt enjoyed cooking, she had prepared all the meals herself, and everybody ate, including the children. So, if it were the food or drink, we would have all been dead.

But it later dawned on me that a few weeks before, she had returned to New York from Jamaica with signs and symptoms of gastroenteritis. She was seen by a doctor across the street from her house who told her she had picked up a bug in Jamaica, and she was prescribed antibiotics. At the time we were leaving New York for Jamaica, my aunt was taking Maalox for stomach burn.

Today I still cannot understand the reason. I am not here to judge anyone as to the real cause of her death.

When my mother visited, she came to my room where I had isolated myself to grieve. I did not want my mother to see me crying. My mother said, "I don't know what to say. I am your birthmother, but Una is closer to you than me, and I don't even know what to tell you. Never mind. This is a shock. When we heard of the death, we thought she had an accident."

I could hardly get my words out, and I could not hold back the tears. I was sobbing uncontrollably whilst at the same time not wanting my birthmother to see that I was grieving so much. More so, when she mentioned that I was closer to Aunt Una than her, my own mother, this heightened the emotions.

I asked my mother if her brother and brother in-law knew auntie had died. She responded, "Yes." She told me that her brother-in-law said, "Anybody can die. Even me standing here can drop dead now."

I asked again, "Was he not shocked to know that she is dead?"

She said, "That is how some people react to death. People grieve in different ways."

There is an old Jamaican saying, "Believe kill and believe cure." On the journey to Jamaica, my aunt had told me, "Marie, my daughter, if anything should happen to me, I do not want to be stringed up to any machine. If I cannot help myself, please let me go. I don't want to be helpless with anybody having to wash and dress me."

I would have been ready and willing to care for her, if I'd had to do so, but time did not enable my aunt to need care for long. This was my first experience being with someone so close this minute and the next minute they were gone. I loved her so much. That day she left us, she took part of me with her. May her dear soul rest in peace.

After Aunt Una's death, I took time off work to get myself together. I worked in a mental institution and feeling the way I did, I needed time to get myself together to keep myself sane. After the funeral, I went back to Jamaica. It was difficult to cope. However, life had to go on, and although I never truly got over this, I had to learn to cope and live without my aunt.

CHAPTER 19

MY MOTHER'S PASSING

My mother's illness was misdiagnosed for years. By the time doctors came to grips with it, she was diagnosed with stage four cancer.

My mother used to prepare cassava starch, which she used on my uniform before the final ironing phase. She sewed the finest clothes and ensured that her children were always smartly dressed. As a result, no one could tell that I only received two school uniforms per semester.

She cooked the most sumptuous traditional meals and was well known for her coconut rung down, sweet potato pudding, fried chicken, and escovieched fish. She was trustworthy and a woman of her word. I was not really impressed with the water boots she gave me to wear when it rained. It was only when I travelled overseas that I saw children in water boots walking in the rain that I had a better understanding of the reason we had these.

My mother migrated to the USA and was living in North America. On one of her trips to Jamaica, she became unwell and was diagnosed with cancer by a Jamaican doctor. It was recommended that she have surgery. At this late stage of the illness, surgery was not of much help, but some of the symptoms were controlled for a while.

Her request was not to go to a nursing home. Instead, she wanted to be cared for in her own home. I visited her regularly to help with her care and treatment. She made me sing her favourite songs several times throughout the course of the day—for example, "Cast all your cares on him;

down at his feet" and "Anytime I don't know what to do I just cast all my cares upon him," and "Father alone will know all about it, Father alone will understand why, cheer up my brother, live in the sunshine."

There were two specific songs that as a family we would sing every morning. These were, "New morning is the love our wakening and uprising prove, through sleep and darkness safely brought our mercies each returning day …" and "Up to the hills where Christ is gone to plead for all his saints, presenting at his father's throne, our songs and our complaints …"

As the illness began getting worse, my mother's physical health started to deteriorate more and more. One night, she told me she was going to die. She asked me to get her a notepad and pen, which she used for writing her funeral programme. Included in the programme was a list of persons she wanted to participate.

One of the church elders, Brother Williams, visited my mother, and she asked for him to give a tribute. In addition, she asked to have lots of flowers. Of her nine children, she asked for her six daughters to carry her casket. On her dying bed, she gave to each daughter a bank book she had kept whilst privately saving for each of us. For every amount of money we sent to our mother, she saved it for us.

I remember asking my mother, "Mama, you are so good. So why are you suffering like this?"

She replied, "Illness does not respect anyone. We are all going to die one day. I asked God for more time. He is now ready for me."

Despite the intensity of the pain, my mother spoke highly of Dr Spence. She described her doctor as being very caring. One of the things that meant a lot to her was that Dr Spence took the time to talk to her.

My mother succumbed to her illness about two years after her diagnosis. She died on the morning of 13 May 2000. My aunt, who was the main carer, on that day described her as fully conscious and alert at the point when she took her last breath. If care, money, and prayer could buy health, she would still be alive today.

When my mother passed away, Brother Williams (her church elder) sent his condolences and apologies that he would not be able to attend the funeral. The reason he gave was that he was traveling to North America. He had no control over his travel plan, as his daughter had already purchased his ticket. Although I felt disappointed, I had to accept it, as I clearly understood the circumstances. I knew my mother had carefully hand-picked her selection of whom she wanted to assist in her funeral plan. Hundreds of funeral programmes were already printed, and it was now too late to change the content.

The day before the funeral, I received a surprise call from Brother Williams. He said, "I will be attending sister Wil's funeral. I will be doing a tribute." I asked what happened with his trip. Brother Williams told me that he went to the airport to check in for his flight, and he was unable to board the flight, as his travel documents had expired. The programme went ahead as my mother had planned it.

CHAPTER 20

MY FATHER'S PASSING

My father Kenneth died suddenly from a stroke in February 2000. He was airlifted via helicopter to KPH Hospital from Port Antonio Hospital by the Jamaica Defence Force in the company of his son. My brother described the lack of care and neglect by health care professionals. He said he had to stretch over the nurse to fix my dad's oxygen mask, which had fallen to one side of his face, and he had to wipe the excess froth from our father's mouth as the nurse sat with her hands folded in the helicopter.

My brother informed me that whilst my father was in the early stages of his admission, my brother was informed by a nurse that the doctor had instructed for my father to get a CT scan done privately. My father had to be transported again in his critical state from the hospital to another facility to get this done. My brother said his worst nightmare was when the nurse demanded payment first before telling him that my father had died.

The delay in assessing treatment did not help the situation, as my father died within a few days of admission. I was in the UK when I received the call that my father had been admitted to hospital, and the nurse told me it was nothing to worry about. By the time I reached home four days later, I was directed to the morgue, where his lifeless body lay on a tray in the refrigerator with an incorrect name on top of the white sheet that his body was wrapped in. When I saw his accident and emergency nursing notes, I was appalled. My father was received at the hospital in a comatose state, yet the nursing notes read " … gentleman, transferred from ... hospital fully conscious and alert in no CV distress ..."

What would it take the admitting nurse to ask a senior to assist if she was not sure what to do? Competency skills seemed to have been lacking in carrying out the assessment for the deteriorating patient, who was already comatose. I now live with the thought of what could have been but was not done. I declared never to work in an area of nursing if I was not able to give the best care possible. A selflessly lived life was struck down quicker than it ought to have been by the lack of care and dignity.

When I looked in the bag he brought into hospital with his belongings and toiletries, every item was unused. This made me question what type of care he received for those four days, lying in bed unable to care for himself, in the back of the ward farthest from the nurses' station. I discussed this with a senior nurse on duty at the time, as I contemplated which basin, washcloth, and soap were used to wash my father when none of his own items was touched. I said, "No wonder he died; the lack of care would have killed him anyway."

The senior nurse laughed at my comment and said, "Newman, you are too funny."

This was not a joke. So, to my fellow nurses and colleagues, thanks to those of you who are showing the six Cs: caring, compassion, commitment, communication, courage, and competence. I implore all of us to give the care that we would wish to receive for ourselves. One of my teachers, Ms Campbell, whilst teaching physical assessment, said, "Always remember, but for the will of God, there go I."

My uncle Bentley (my mother's brother) visited whilst I was on holiday with my sister Ve and her son in Jamaica. When Uncle Bentley arrived, he began sharing experiences about my dad with my sister's son. He said, "Your grandfather was a good man. He always welcomed everyone to his house. He was always willing to share what he had. He provided work for at least one family member from each household in the community. He was hardworking, reliable, and honest. This is the one man I could trust. People like your grandfather don't exist anymore. He gave to others without expecting anything in return."

I took the notes and shared some emotions with my sister Ve. I told Ve that this was exactly how I want to remember my father, and that I wanted this quote for my book.

She said, "Do not worry, I am sure if you ask him again, the response would be the same. He was stating facts which will remain the same, but if it was false information, this would change."

Even though I planned my journey to go home and help to take care of my father, time did not allow me to do so. He was too unwell to wait for me. I was devastated at the news of his death as

I was packing to leave the UK. Instead of going home to be his nurse, I was now going home to bury my father.

I met a young man called Eva as I exited the arrival hall. Eva walked up to me and gave me a hug. He said, "Marie, if I feel this way, I can only imagine how you feel."

I swallowed my saliva as I felt the deepest sense of sadness, the choking feeling in my throat, and the unexplainable butterflies as a void encapsulated everything around me. I could not bear the thought that my father was really gone.

Eva carried on with the conversation, saying, "I can remember as a young boy, after my father died, Mass Kenneth [referring to my father] called me and gave me a job to move lumber-plant pots from one place to the next. On my payday, the only thing your father said to me was 'Take care of your mother.' I can only think that the job was given to me so that I could provide for my family, since my father was no longer around. It was not because I could do the work. Basically, I could not, as I was too young to do any of the work that the workmen were doing. The job I was given to do was really nothing to do. It was a way to make a living for the family."

My vocabulary is limited in finding the right words to explain the feeling when I arrived home at my father's house in the cool hills of Durham that night. The wind was blowing gently and all else was at peace. The entire community was in mourning, as the people gathered around in a vigil. I walked to the back of the house. People were in the kitchen preparing fritters, dumplings, soup, fried fish, and chocolate tea.

A feeling of loneliness, sadness, and emptiness was all around. There were people visiting our home, and my distressed mother was present to greet me. My mother anxiously tried to explain what had happened. I was inconsolable. She spoke about my father telling her that if he died, a particular worker knew what had happened to the missing animals, including two goats, and that he only had one blood pressure tablet left.

I said to my mother, "So you checked and gave him the tablet, right?"

She replied, "No."

I told my mother to go and look for the tablet container. I followed my mother as she walked towards the bedroom. My mother opened the drawer and handed me a small medicine container labelled *Aldomet 500 mg, take one tablet daily*. One tablet was left in the container.

I asked my mother again, "Why did you not give him his tablet if he said this to you?"

She responded, "I did not take him seriously, until he fell and wasn't able to get back on the bed. That was when I called for help."

My father once told me that, "When someone calls you, always respond. This could be their last call and your opportunity to help save a life."

For this reason, I never ignored anyone, more so my patients, as I always thought this could be their last call. This was certainly my father's last call, and of course my mother missed the opportunity to realise that this was so.

Although I hadn't expected my father to live forever, neither did I expect death to be so sudden. I was broken, and it took me years to accept this impermissible act and to learn to live again and enjoy my own life. I had such great plans, as I'd looked forward to birthdays and spending holidays with my parents.

I visited one of my father's few surviving friends in hospital, and during our conversation, he said, "People like your dad are hard to find these days. He was one in a million. He was a man who everyone in the community looked up to.

He was highly respected, yet he was so humble, dedicated, and kind. People like your dad don't exist anymore."

His comment was similar to that of my uncle and many older people in the community where my father lived. This gave me some reassurance that although my father was gone, the memories lived on for those whose lives he had touched.

CHAPTER 21

A BIG DECISION

Over time, whatever came my way, I had to learn not to give up easily anymore. I had to learn to be strong-willed, assertive, positive, and proactive.

My first work experience in a mental-health setting was totally different from anything I could have imagined. I would go beyond the call of duty, but nothing I did could ever please my supervisor. She even reported that she was not getting any support from her nurses. Her complaints lead to the matron transferring me to another unit.

There has been and there still is a growing trend of blame culture as well as blame for others' errors in the workplace. Probably we need some type of managers who are "trained to solve the case." Usually, the truth comes out, but most times it is late and sometimes too late. False allegations were daunting, especially when they landed on the table of managers who were not equipped to deal with such atrocities, often leading to conscious or unconscious bias.

Following my move to my new ward, the admission unit, Sister Satchell—my manager in Jamaica at the time—told me that the matron had called to check up on me and to find out how I was doing. She said, "I told her as far as I am concerned, you are a damn good nurse, and I want to keep you on my ward." This was a relief to know that I had a manager who not only understood me but acknowledged my work and competence and valued me as a staff member.

Within three months, I was given a promotion to be the interim ward manager. When my manager returned from her extended leave, I was promoted to the position of ward manager on LG ward. At first, I refused the job offer, because I was happy to go back to my role as staff nurse and continue working with my manager. I did not feel confident about taking on the responsibility of being ward manager for such a large unit. When my manager told me that with my level of competence, I could manage any ward, this touched my heart. So, with the encouragement and support from Sister Satchell and Matron Riley, in the end, I accepted the challenge.

It did not take long for me to learn the ropes, and I was able to build an excellent working relationship with all the staff. According to well-known entrepreneur Richard Branson: "If you are offered a job and you don't know how to do it, take the job and learn how to do it."

Though it was difficult at times, I had to learn how to cope and how to work with stakeholders at all levels. I was called "baby nurse" by some of the staff in my job. However, when the staff got to know me and I got to know them, work life was even greater.

I met nurses from other countries who came to work in the Bellevue Mental Hospital, some of whom questioned me as to why I was registered with the Nursing and Midwifery Council (NMC) United Kingdom and had not taken a job offer to work in the UK. Whilst I was working with these nurses, they often mentioned how they wished they'd had the opportunity to be registered with the NMC, as this was their intention. However, at that time, I was only interested in visiting the UK to train as an occupational therapist and fulfil a childhood dream to be more fluent in the English language. While in school, I was told English originated in England, hence one of my favourite pastimes was to listen to the BBC World News every day.

I gave this some thought, and after many ponderings, I decided to migrate to the UK. My interest in occupational therapy was a dream that was never explored in the end. Instead of studying occupational therapy, I accepted a job offer to work in a nursing home in Dorset.

CHAPTER 22

THE JOURNEY FROM JAMAICA TO ENGLAND

I travelled on Air Jamaica to London Heathrow Airport. The flight seemed endless. I imagined what England would be like and how I would adjust to my new environment.

I could have said I missed my family, but that would be too much of an understatement. I felt as if I had left half of myself behind. It was too much of a brave decision to leave my immediate family of five children and my husband behind. Even though the flight was full, there was a sense of loneliness and bewilderment. I felt empty and alone, as this was the first time travelling without my family.

I positioned myself on an aisle next to the window as I glanced at my boarding pass to ensure that I was sitting in my allocated seat. An announcement came over the intercom, so I followed the instructions from a crew member to ensure my hand luggage was put in the overhead compartment, my handbag was under the seat in front of me, and my seat belt was fastened. I whispered a prayer for safe travel and arrival at my destination.

Looking out the window in a daze, I watched as the plane accelerated along the runway for take-off and gradually climbed to cruising altitude. In the distance, towards the ground, everything looked miniature. I gazed through the window until the land disappeared from my sight, and at this point all that was visible was what appeared to be massive clumps of white clouds.

The Paradigm That Changed My Life Forever

The ride was initially smooth, but mid-journey, it became quite bumpy. This was not as turbulent as the throbbing of my heartbeat. During the journey, the pilot announced a few times that the airplane was "going through areas of turbulence. All passengers must stay in your seats with seat belts securely fastened until the 'fasten seat belt' sign is switched off." I recollected my past encounters with nature, as it was now taking a toll in new dimensions.

After nine and a half hours, the airplane landed safely at Heathrow Airport in the United Kingdom. I hastened to join other passengers in applauding by clapping our hands. This is a known custom for Jamaicans to show appreciation and gratitude for safe travel.

After instructions were given to disembark the aircraft, I joined the queue of passengers standing in the aisle of the airplane waiting to exit. As I walked to the immigration area, my mind was flooded with distracting thoughts, such as, "Why am I in the UK? What is going to happen? How could I have left my children behind? Am I going crazy?"

I waited in the immigration line for all the security checks to be completed to enter the United Kingdom. I rubbed my hands over my clothes to dry my wet palms before giving my passport to the officer. Questions were hurled at me by an immigration officer who was staring me in the eyes, such as, "What's the purpose of your visit? Did you get a work permit in Jamaica?" I knew all was well when the immigration officer said, "Mrs Newman, welcome to the United Kingdom" as he handed me my passport and directed me to the baggage hall.

I thought it is not too bad after all. He sounded very polite. I said, "Thank you, sir." Then I walked gingerly through the hustle and bustle of passengers looking for their luggage. Suitcases and bags were being pulled from the luggage belt. Some of the passengers collected their luggage and could be seen pushing trolleys along through the "Nothing to Declare" zone.

Upon exit from immigration, I saw a vast number of people of multicultural origins in the arrival-hall waiting area. Some were holding up placards, which captured my attention. Amidst the crowd I saw two men standing next to each other at the waiting gallery. One was holding a card with *Marie Newman* written in bold black writing. Unknown to me, these two men, Mr P and his business partner, were my prospective bosses.

I walked towards them with butterflies in my stomach. Although I had previously had telephone conversations with Mr P, the director of the company I would be working for, this was the first time we were meeting face to face. I walked towards the two men to make myself known, thinking of the best way to make my greeting sound cheerful, as I was feeling overly anxious now. I said, "Hello my name is Marie Newman." I tried to keep a brave face as I struggled to hold back the tears and hoped it would not give my fear away.

Mr P and his business partner both responded in a bright and polite manner. They directed me to the airport car park. Both men eagerly helped with my luggage as we walked.

When we got into the car, I was assured by Mr P that I would be arriving at my destination (Dorset) within a couple of hours. The reality of being in the United Kingdom started to hit me hard. I could not stop thinking that I was in a foreign country travelling in a car with two male strangers. My thoughts were focused on the realities that were unfolding as well as the uncertainties of what was to come. Nonetheless, I engaged in intermittent conversation as we travelled the country roads to the nursing home in Dorset where I would be working.

I was surprised by the architecture of some buildings, as I had great expectations, even though I did not know what the general scenery would be like. My imagination changed to the realism of what this side of the world was about to reveal to me. I was seeing what was real and what was just a myth, as well as what was about to change.

I watched herds of sheep on the hillside as we passed the farm areas. It was a pleasure to see the uniqueness, the natural and stunning beauty of the countryside. One sight that made a lasting impact on the journey to Sherborne was of one of the scenic wonders of the world, Stonehenge. This is a prehistoric monument consisting of a ring of stones uniquely shaped; it is regarded as a British cultural icon. After about two hours, we arrived at the nursing home where I was going to work.

This book was started in May 1999, when I first came to England. I struggled with fear and anxiety as I went into overthinking mode. I tried different coping mechanisms, such as talking to friends, singing, listening to music, going for a walk to Sherborne town centre, visiting the matron's home, and shopping—even shopping for things that I did not need just as a treat. But nothing helped. I resorted to writing, as it was the only way I could control my thoughts from all the internal and external dilemmas surrounding me at the time.

I started keeping a diary of events as my work and personal life began changing rapidly, in many ways. I did not know what to do, and writing became my saving grace. Writing was a cleft for me, and I hid myself in it.

My expectations of England were quite different from my real experience of England. For example, having listened to the British Broadcasting Corporation (BBC) world news every morning whilst living in Jamaica, I was expecting to meet people with similar British accents as I heard on the BBC news. Instead, I came across a wide variety of accents and languages. I met people of diverse origins, some of whom left a lasting impact.

There were times when I had to keep pushing to motivate myself to complete tasks, as things were becoming too much for me and I was losing confidence in myself. At times, I felt as if I was not going to make it, as the paths chosen seemed blocked, with too many hurdles to cross.

Along the way, I learned that it is always better to have an open mind rather than harbour stereotypes. The grass only seemed greener from a distance in the areas I valued the most.

Looking back, I could have done more research before taking such a big step. Once I started, it was difficult to go back, especially since my job in Jamaica would no longer be available. If I returned, I would be expected to start all over from being a staff nurse.

I had moved from working in one of the largest mental health institutions in the Caribbean to work in a nursing home in England. The entire bed capacity in the nursing home was nothing compared the ward I had managed in Jamaica. Initially, I was interested in pursuing a career in occupational therapy in the UK, as at that time there was only one qualified occupational therapist in the entire mental health hospital where I worked in Jamaica. It was evident there was a demand in this area, and I thought it would be a good idea, but this was not to be. After discussing this with a colleague, I decided to take a job in an area in which I already had training and experience.

Working in the nursing home was challenging, especially re-learning how to work in a similar profession, as work life here was so different from my previous job. One of the most interesting areas was the differences in work cultures, coupled with people dynamics. The work on its own was never an issue.

CHAPTER 23

ANOTHER TRAGIC DEATH

On a visit I made to Jamaica, my nephew Taren approached me about not being able to gain employment after completion of his course in agriculture. He told me that he had applied for many jobs and had not received a single response. We met to discuss possible options.

We went job-hunting and hand-delivered applications to the Ministry of Agriculture, Rural Agricultural Development Authority, and the Forest Department. Within two weeks, Taren told me he had received invites for interviews for all his applications. As he requested, I did some coaching with him prior to the interviews. This worked well for Taren, as he humbled himself to my novice coaching.

Following his interviews, he was offered a job with the Ministry of Agriculture as a plant quarantine officer at the Norman Manley International Airport Jamaica after having worked for a short period at the Ministry of Social Security as a bookkeeper. On one of his faithful workdays, Taren was driving on the airport road to carry out his work duties as usual. Taren was involved in a serious motor vehicle accident that claimed his life. His two work colleagues who were travelling with him survived the accident.

The memory of the trauma of Taren's death often comes back at times, as if the incident happened yesterday. Taren was one of my closest and dearest nephews. He started working with the Ministry of Agriculture one year before his death. At the start of the funeral service, whilst well-wishers and family were sharing their tributes, a gentleman in the audience got up and asked if he could say something.

The gentleman said that he had gone to the airport two weeks before Taren's passing to clear duty for flowers that were imported for his workplace. He said he came across Taren for the first time, and Taren's excellent customer service skills as a plant quarantine officer left some passionate memories with him. He said that on reading the *Jamaican Sunday Gleaner*, he was taken aback when he saw Taren's photo in the death column.

He further said that although he noted that it would take him over two hours to drive from Kingston to Portland, the distance did not deter him, as he could not have missed the funeral. He wanted to pay his last respects and to share his brief but lasting encounter with Taren. For me, this is how I would want to be remembered when I die. I cherished the memories of Taren and the relationship we shared.

CHAPTER 24

LIVING AND WORKING IN ENGLAND

I experienced racism in different aspects of my working life, even from people of similar culture. Some of these racist attacks were subtle, but others were open. I was asked questions such as, "What made you leave your country to come here?" and "Why are you here?" I was called "black" and "chocolate." I woke up one morning with my glass windows all clouded with smashed eggs. Whilst I was walking on the street, children picked up snow and threw it at me, and one boy even deliberately threw stones and smashed my window.

At the time the latter happened, I was sitting in my living room when the window glass shattered next to me. I called the police, and this case was eventually resolved. The young boy's parents replaced the window and brought their son to hand me a bunch of flowers. He apologized for breaking the window, and I accepted. He was just a young boy.

One evening, as I walked home from work, I was just in time to rescue my daughter after she was surrounded by eleven girls from her school, two of whom were pointing in her face and threatening to fight her, with others cheering them on. The girls were shouting at her, "You think you are clever." As I was about to call the police, they ran away.

My experiences with some of the staff at the nursing home were good, but others were not so good. Some persons made it their duty to negate others. Blaming culture was not to be, however.

This was often used as a weapon, and allegations were made without evidence at the expense of others' time and emotions. The following scenario supports this claim.

In June 1999, while tending to a patient in her bedroom, I heard a stumbling sound at the rear door. I saw two Caucasian healthcare workers, one peeping through the door whilst the other pulled the window curtain. They seemed disappointed when they could not find anything to report, as the patient complimented me for the care delivered that day.

This incident pulled me out of my comfort zone and motivated me to look for another job. At times, I could not help but wonder how people could be so unkind. I encouraged these staff members to develop themselves if they so desired. I explained my course of training and the process of becoming a qualified nurse.

One of the staff applied and went for the interview to do adult nursing, and I supported some of the healthcare assistants to achieve their National Vocational Qualification (NVQ). By the time I was planning to move on, the staff had all taken a different view of me. But being the only black person working in the environment, it was difficult for me. Healthcare work can be rewarding, but also stressful.

Personally, I do not feel people should spend time at work frustrating their colleagues. There is a saying, "Misery loves company," and one must be politically astute and diplomatic to survive in today's work environment. It can be frustrating working with individuals who are instigators for trouble without any relevant or factual reason to do so. It took me a lot of wisdom and understanding to balance work and personal life.

A colleague of mine had joined the nursing home facility where I was working. Initially, I did not foresee any problem and was happy for her to come and work. When the director asked me to apply for the deputy manager's position, I shared this with my colleague, believing she would be happy for me. I learned the hard way to be careful who to share successes with. I had to come to an awareness of what I needed to share with friends and family and what I did not need to share, as well as their purpose in my life. After sharing what I thought was good news with my colleague, she wrote on the notice board: "What is the criteria for a deputy matron?"

I believe people behave the way they do for different reasons. This was beyond my imagination. I had all good intentions in mind, supporting and encouraging others to develop themselves, and these persons could still turn around and maliciously try to cause unnecessary issues. By nature, and personality-wise, I tend to listen a lot more than engaging in verbalism. This is innate from early childhood, so I try to think of what I say and how my words make sense to other people as well as the aftereffect. With all best intentions, words can be interpreted differently, sometimes just to suit someone's own preconceived ideas.

The nurse said that she was dual-qualified. What is the use of midwifery in a nursing home? These clients were all over the age of 65 years. Having a qualification of adult and mental health seemed more applicable to the role of deputy matron, as some clients had physical and mental health problems. My thoughts were disturbed about this situation, because I was focusing on other people's views. Thinking too much on others' views of me determined how I was feeling and reacting.

I decided that I wanted to move to a more specialised area of work where I could learn new skills and aspire in my nursing role. When I shared this with my manager at the nursing

The Paradigm That Changed My Life Forever

home, she gave me a *Nursing Times* magazine and informed me that she would like to give me a reference before she moved on to another job offer. I searched through the job advertisements in the *Nursing Times,* and I came across an advertisement at St Peter's Hospital for a "recovery nurse."

I shared with a friend that I wanted to work for this hospital. My friend gave me some insightful information as to the location and how this could be a possibility. I talked myself into doing things and worked towards them, learning to be more aware of what I asked for. In the end, I convinced myself to put in my application for the role of recovery nurse. My father often said, "Make everything you do a good gesture. Do not trample anyone whilst climbing your ladder. You may meet them on your way when it's time to come down."

In early January 2000, I received a letter confirming that I was shortlisted for the job in the National Health Service. At my interview for the post of recovery nurse, one of the questions a panel member asked was, "Why did you apply for this job?"

My response was, "I saw the job in the *Nursing Times*, and I said to myself, *This job is for me. This is the kind of job I have been looking for. This is what I want to do.*"

You may ask, did I get the job to work at St Peter's Hospital? The answer is yes, I did.

I worked at this facility for over seven consecutive years and moved up the ranks from a D-grade to F-grade and even worked in the capacity of a G-grade liaison nurse. (D-grade at the time was a lower-level nurse, E a more senior nurse, F a deputy manager, and G a team manager or ward manager). What is yours can be yours if you set your goals and work towards achieving them.

I had the experience of working with some excellent managers in the NHS, some of whom helped me to develop in many different aspects. A new staff nurse, Emmanuel, told me that Marcia, the manager, wrote in his acceptance offer letter, "I will not be available on your first start date, but you will be working with a competent registered nurse, Marie Newman, who will be carrying out your induction." I was humbled when he showed me the letter. It was rewarding to know that I was valued by my manager, and more so that she trusted my competence. For this reason, I was at my best when doing Emmanuel's induction.

I told myself that no matter what, if I could not improve my standards, I would never allow anything or anyone to make me lower the standards that I already possessed. My aim was to deliver the best care and offer my support to others where I could. When I left my first job, I realized that staff, even though they might not show or say it, felt supported. This was evident in cards received from staff. I received one card signed by seventeen staff members. Over 90 percent of staff mentioned the words *grateful for your support and knowledge shared, you will do well wherever you go,* and *it was nice* or *lovely working with you.*

At my leaving, it became known that staff even went out of their way to call my daughter to ask her what I liked. My daughter was told to keep this a secret, and she did. I only learned about this when I received a Harrods bag with a bottle of Knowing perfume and a card full of lasting compliments. I asked the staff how they knew that this perfume was my favourite. I was indeed humbled by their efforts when I was told by a nurse, "We did our homework."

It was great knowing that the little things I did without taking any note meant so much to staff. At the same time, it was imperative for me to know that no matter how good a person may be, it may not always be possible to have a rapport with everyone. What mattered to me most was having respect and a good working relationship with everyone.

CHAPTER 25

MALICIOUS COMPLAINTS

I experienced two distinct malicious complaints during my nursing career. In both cases, whilst trying to coin an allegation to defame me, they were writing the allegations about their own lack of competence. For the second one, I sat in an investigation room listening to questions hurled at me. I had no defence except my own words and that the libel was untrue.

The way the allegation was put forward, only the experience, knowledge, understanding, and expert ability of the panel could find the hidden truth, but grace, faith, and hope intervened and pleaded the facts on my behalf. I took to the stand to answer panel members' questions. After the deliberation, I was called back into the room for the verdict. I was told that from the eleven persons called in for witness testimony, there was nothing against me. Therefore, the case was upheld. When asked about a counter claim, I declined. I felt like there was nothing to do, as grace, faith, and hope were already covering the facts and intervening on by behalf. For me, leaving people to their conscience was the best thing to do.

There were many times at work when I felt invisible, as my opinion was undervalued. If I was quiet, I was too passive and was not contributing to the conversation; yet when I did contribute, I was either ignored or made to feel stupid by the undermining comments. All it took was one person starting a negative comment, and this could take off like a rocket. Sometimes I would just whisper "Lord have mercy."

Everything that happened, even when I was not present, was blamed on. Me. I prayed before I would leave my house, when I reached work, and when I would leave work. What was surprising was staff who approached me after I left the job and said, "Marie, it was only after you left us that we knew who we had. Will you come back and work with us?"

CHAPTER 26

THE FAILED DRIVING TESTS

I passed my theory driving test the first time. However, I failed my practical driving test more than ten times. There were days when I felt so discouraged that I wanted to give up.

As I kept trying, I kept failing. Each time, I would pay for a patch of twenty lessons and a double lesson on the day of the test. On one occasion, I failed on three points. When my instructor asked the examiner "What did Marie do? She is capable of doing the same as any other person who passed," the examiner responded, "a little bitty." The examiner had instructed me to drive straight unless he asked me to turn. As I was driving, I came up on a one-way sign, so I asked the examiner, "Should I turn left?" His reasoning was that I should not have asked; I should have just turned left if it is a one-way street ahead.

Feedback from another examiner was, "You went near the curb."

My question to this examiner was, "Did I touch the curb?"

His response was, "No, you just went near."

Following one of my tests, I sat in the car with the examiner waiting for my feedback, as he was taking a long time, I glanced over to see what he was writing. The examiner was counting the errors. He added two ticks for mirror, then he again counted along the tick boxes with his pen in hand. In addition to the first two ticks for mirror, he added another two ticks, making it four points for mirror. He counted again and added more points. He then added up again and his total was now one point over the limit for minor faults to gain a pass.

My instructor intervened again and asked, "What did Marie do wrong this time?"

The examiner told him that I did not pass the test.

My instructor replied, "She can do as much as any other person who has passed the test."

It was at this point that my instructor advised me to contact the Driving License Agency (DVLA). I wrote to the DVLA regarding the number of times that I had failed my driving test despite being a full PPV licensed driver in another country. Following this, I booked another driving test. On the day of the test, I had just finished a night shift on a busy acute psychiatric ward. I had prepared for the test several times before, taking days off and annual leave for practice sessions, and in addition up to two hours of lessons before the test. After all this, I still failed, so to me at this point it made no sense making the extra effort. Today was very different. I was not doing any pre-preparation.

My instructor accompanied me to the Driving Test Centre as usual. On arrival, we were met by a new examiner, a tall, older-looking, medium-built Caucasian gentleman. He checked my documents and instructed me to meet him in the car park. He told me that as the car park was empty, I should do a reverse park in one of the bays. As I reversed into the bay, the instructor asked me: "Do you want to do anything else?" To this I responded, "No."

Following this, I was instructed by the examiner to drive to the main road, follow the signs, and drive along, taking the instructions from him. After about thirty-five minutes of driving, he instructed me to drive back to the Test Centre.

When we arrived at the Test Centre, the examiner instructed me to pull up somewhere safe. As the car came to a stop, the examiner said, "Congratulations. I see no reason to fail you."

Had I given up, I would not be able to drive in the UK today. So, keep trying. Today or tomorrow or the next day may not be your day to pass, but your day will eventually come if you keep trying.

CHAPTER 27

UNIVERSITY STUDIES

The thought of attending an overseas university and paying fees was daunting. I did not know how I would cope, but I took the chance. I often asked myself, where would my help come from? But with Christ in the vessel, I was able to smile at the storm, as he provided me with the right people who provided the right support.

It was during one of my saddest moments that someone sent me this quote: "My help comes from above ... I looked up to the hills, but where does my help come from? My help comes from the Lord, who made heaven and earth. He will not let you be defeated. He who guards you never sleeps." (Psalms 121).

It was as if this was the moment of transformation for me. I could no longer wait for the perfect time to attend university, since there might never be an ideal time. I sent in an application for the degree in nursing studies at Buckinghamshire University College, United Kingdom. Following a successful interview, I was offered a place at the University Chalfont Campus UK. After some negotiation with the finance team, I was offered the opportunity to set up a payment plan with the university, as I was self-funding.

At the same time, I was funding my daughter Seon's fees. She was also a student at this university. If she had known of the sacrifice, she would have at least made an effort to hand in her assignments, which she failed to do. The payments were deducted from my bank account monthly with the terms of payment to end at the completion date of our courses.

I have always admired my parents for their self-sufficiency, and as such I believed that if I wanted something, I had to be willing to make the sacrifice. Therefore, I had to pay the cost for what I needed. Consequently, when I was given the option to pay monthly, I did not hesitate to take up this offer with gratitude.

As the course progressed, I became more and more concerned about my grades. Although, I was passing the modules, my grades were not good. First I thought I must be doing something wrong. Assignments submitted for marking were merely scoring a C or a C+. I felt as if I was being capped at this, as almost all my tutors were giving similar grades. Although I was grateful for just passing, at the same time, I was thinking I must be capable of doing better.

It reached a stage where I had enough of C grades. I decided to have a discussion with one of my professors, Dr K. E., regarding the reason I was not achieving at a higher level, and to find out what I needed to do to improve my current grades. Dr K. E. suggested I send him an email with my draft work, which I did. He questioned one of the words I had used in my assignment. I told him this was an English word which I had come across in the Oxford Dictionary. He emailed his feedback, highlighting the area he said could be taken out if the assignment went over the required word limit. At the end of the message, he commented, "Good luck."

In another review, he mentioned that he had looked up the word and *it was an English word that was used in the right context.*

Following receipt of the feedback, I proceeded to complete the assignment. I emailed my friend Professor Clement Lambert to ask him to proofread my work before the final submission. I was still unsure about the "good luck" comment that I had received from Dr K. E. Initially, Dr Lambert did not respond, so I made further contact with him to find out if he was in receipt of my email. Eventually, his response was, "There is nothing wrong with the article. Just hand it in. If I had marked this work, it would have been awarded an A."

I did not think Dr Lambert was obligated to read my work, but with the C grades, I was worried about getting the usual capped C. I was at least expecting some sort of feedback on the areas that could be improved.

Anyway, I submitted my paper, as the deadline for submission was fast approaching. For this particular piece of work, I did not get the usual C; I received my first A. The overall result for the degree was a 2:1 (second class honours upper division). "To God be the glory, great things he has done" through the people who supported me as well as the intuition to seek support from my lecturer and for his understanding in listening to my concerns.

In my younger years, I used to think people I associated with, such as friends and family, shared the same feelings I did. So, if I asked for support from my family, I believed I should get it in the same way as I would for them. However, I soon learned that I had to help myself, and the latter part of this comment became one of my main challenges. Simple things that would take a few minutes took me days due to my poor IT skills. I was faced with excuse after excuse when I asked others for help. Sometimes there was no response; other times, it was more of "What do you think?" or "Oh! That's simple, just do it," or "I wish I could help, but I don't have time. I am doing my own work. At least I am being paid for this," or "Email it to me, I will have a look if I can."

Sometimes when I asked a family member to listen to a sentence and tell me if it made sense, I received no response. To put this straight, I was simply being ignored and given the cold shoulder. I ended up purchasing a book on basic IT skills, but instead of using the book to help myself, I gave the book to someone who was struggling a little more than me.

I began thinking and doing things differently after not being successful with getting the support I was seeking. As a result of the change in thinking, experiences began to unfold in my favour. I was able to make changes that helped me not only be more self-sufficient but also to develop a network of the right people with whom I could share my experiences.

Changing my outlook on life did not change the reality that I very often found myself in a friendly as well as an intimidating atmosphere. However, what was crucial now was the awareness that my development depended on me. The experiences, environment, and people I associated with, how I saw my road, is how my journey was created.

I drove to Bucks University following directions on a piece of paper I had printed from Google Maps to find the location. Directions and finding places had always been a major issue for me. I did not like trying new things, but my failures and mistakes became an opportunity to grow.

I had learned to read maps with the help of Linda, a colleague at work. Linda took quality time to demonstrate how to read the road map of the United Kingdom step by step, as there was no sat navigation system at the time. The people I expected support from were not the ones who supported me through my journey.

When I asked my best friend and soulmate for help, things started out very well. I was all excited and pleased with the initial support to formulate some of my interview questions for my research.

However, he stopped before I understood what I was doing. As this was my first experience conducting a research paper, I was left more confused than when I started. No begging, pleading, or compromise would help.

When I saw that this was not to be, I came to realize that if I was going to make it, I had to look at other options to complete the course. I remember a favourite quote that my father copied: "The heights of great men reached and kept, but they while their companion slept were toiling upwards in the night" (author unknown). There were some phrases that my father often used, including "Use night to patch day. Work while you can. Eat when you are healthy."

The thought that my mother called me "Hope" was all beginning to make perfect sense. With this hopeful feeling, the motivation started coming back. I was more determined now to keep the confidence going, as I could not afford to fail the course. I was paying my own university fees, working a full-time job, a mother of five children, and the primary breadwinner for the family. This played back at me as I made the decision that I was not going to reach the last lap of this academic pursuit and give up when I was almost at the point of completion. My mother blamed us, her children, for her not finishing her teacher course, and I did not want to do the same to my children.

Based on my experiences, I believed that when helping a learner, educators should not take for granted that they know the learner's needs. Individuals learn in different ways. I was often told what to do rather than being asked what I needed help with, and most of the help that was given was what I already knew.

I feel learners should be asked where they need help the most. It was only when the right support and resources were available that I could truly meet my goals. Being the learner listening to the teacher/supervisor/supporter is just as important as the teacher listening to me to make sense of my needs.

Attitude was another major factor that impacted my learning and development. When emotions got in the way, it made things more difficult for me. When I was not going anywhere with my research, my anxieties and frustrations set in. I had to think quickly, as the university deadline for work submission was fast approaching.

I found support from Jill Aitkens, my principal lecturer at Bucks University. She was like a penlight in a dark learning tunnel. The greatest feeling was knowing that I had someone willing to listen to me. If only I had thought of this before, my study life would probably have been much easier. As Jill took the time out of her busy schedule to show me the ropes, she guided me in the right direction to draft the research framework needed to complete the master's course of study. She was very welcoming and approachable, and she gave me the reassurance that it was possible for me to complete my master's.

I met with Jill in her office for review of my work. She explained how to progress with my work, and I had follow-up appointments to review my progress with the assignment. Jill helped me to further reinforce my hope. The anxiety subsided, and my tears became laughter as the work got much easier when I understood what I needed to do.

I spent night after night in the library reading, researching, and writing references while trying to stay awake to complete my work. At times, I found myself writing the same thing multiple times, writing scribbles and sometimes not able to make sense of my own writing. Sometimes when I read my own writing, it all seemed incoherent. The thought was, *Oh, how I wish I could find that one capable person who could just proofread my work.* Sometimes while writing, I was half asleep and half awake. I kept scribbling along, as tiredness and sleep were overpowering me. This was in conjunction with my home responsibilities.

I wanted to give up and go to bed like everyone else in the house, but I remembered Ram, another lecturer at Bucks University, telling me in one of his classes, "Stay awake now, and you can sleep all you want once you have passed the course." So many nights, I stayed up throughout the night at the computer station working on my project. My focus now was to keep awake to complete the work. On many occasions, I fell asleep in the library. As I dreamt about my work, it was as if I could hear Ram's voice, in my half-asleep state, saying, "Stay awake now." The end result was successful completion of the course followed by graduation.

Despite these efforts, there were times when I still felt as if I was not making the progress that was expected. I had so many different modes of motivation. I could be good and raring to go in the morning and struggling to write a paragraph in the afternoon. I would go to the refrigerator many times during the night looking for food to relieve my stress or to avoid facing the assignment. I engaged in unnecessary chores around the house: cleaning, washing, ironing, and folding clothes. I would often sit and just overthink. Therefore, procrastination took a large chunk of my time as I struggled to keep up with the work.

In 2017, I approached a clinical educator regarding my professional development plan to return to education and work at the university. He introduced me to one of the most phenomenal women I had ever met: Associate Professor Margaret Rioga at Buckinghamshire New University. I was impressed by the qualities I saw in Margaret's rapport with students and staff alike. I started teaching as a practice-based partner on the alert course as well as getting involved in mental-health formative assessment for BSc students whilst doing a refresher course in education for the NMC-approved postgraduate certificate in education (PGCE).

Of significance, I will mention my progress on this course. I scored all As except for one paper for which I received a fail. I had thought that was going to be my best grade. The results truly traumatized me, and for the first time I knew what depression felt like. I was saddened that I had put in so much effort. It was not like I felt infallible. If I knew I did not do my work, I would not have had any great expectations. I wanted to appeal, but I was told that I couldn't, and I did not know much about the academic role of student services.

So, I resorted to seeking advice from the Learning and Development Unit. I will not mention names here, but I was very grateful for your feedback, your reassurance, and your kind and thoughtful words. It was this feedback that lifted my spirit when you read those pages and I asked you to read another few and you did. It was a good feeling to know that the work made sense to somebody.

I decided to resubmit my work, as upon reflection, resubmission was not the end of the world, and I did not come this far to leave like this. Moreover, it would be devastating to fail a course that I had passed at a higher level before. Given below is a nugget of the feedback:

Julia shared her wealth of knowledge, skills and experience and showed me the value of being an efficient educator. One of the most admirable qualities was the art of listening, showing compassion, and acknowledging diversity. She has certainly left a legacy and has passed the baton on.

On completion of this course, I was offered a post as a practice educator in the NHS. I continued to work at the university as an associate lecturer. It was at this university whilst standing in the reception area that I met up with my course leader, who had taught me on the course. She said, "What are you doing here?" I told my past course leader that I was working as an associate lecturer. During our conversation, she said, "I am so happy for you. Marie, you know something, I could see this in you."

I applied for a senior lecturer post at the university in early 2020 and started my substantive post working as a senior lecturer on 1 May 2021. It has not been easy, and all is not perfect. I am learning every day, but I finally made it. I may have struggled too much and worked too hard for what I wanted, but it was well worth the struggle.

CHAPTER 28

THE WAKE-UP CALL

I was surfing Facebook when I saw an RIP notification under a friend's page. Mrs Christian, one of my first-grade teachers in all-age school, had passed away. When I saw this, I thought it was time to finish this book.

I saw Mrs Christian in 2010 at my first school in Cooper's Hill when I had gone there to visit with my sister Ve. I had discussed my intent to complete the writing of this book with Mrs Christian. I allowed malingering to take the better part of me; I kept saying I was going to finish, but I could never get myself to do so. The challenges are real--juggling home life, children, and grandchildren with work and the unnecessary atrocities that come along with it, especially the circumstances over which I had no control.

In April 2012, I saw Mrs Christian again, and I mentioned to her that I was still writing the book. I know deep down I was struggling. Mrs Christian, with her usual diplomatic and tactful response, said, "Yes, Marie, please do so. I would love to read the book."

Mrs Christian reading the book is not going to be possible now. Her death was an awakening. It occurred to me that with all the time and energy wasted, I should now write and publish the book. It still took me another five years, as reality hit back at me in 2020 when I heard that Ms Spence, another of my past teachers, had passed away. A few months before this, I was on holiday with my daughter in Jamaica when we ran into Ms

Spence. The first thing she asked my daughter was, "Did your mother tell you about our story?"

Then one of my high-school classmates informed me that Mr Brent Harris, my former geography tutor who taught me to write essays in high school, had passed away. I thought to myself, *Enough is enough. The time is now or never.* I have missed out on three persons I know would have had an interest in reading this book. The Covid-19 pandemic was the final wake-up for me, reminding me that the time to do anything is now, as there is no guarantee of tomorrow. With my heroes in mind, the value of time could not be underestimated.

224

CHAPTER 29

SUMMARY

I hope there will be a time when our voices can be heard without having to worry.

As a black person in the UK, life has had its advantages and disadvantages. The limits in my life were always and will only be those I set for myself. Not every teacher I met in academic institutions supported me, but for those who did, I am grateful. Words cannot express this. For the few who did not, it was still a learning experience. I sought what I needed, and I found what I needed.

It was important to set goals and to have a structured plan as to how to achieve the goals, but it was not only more important to carry out the actions, there was also a sense of relief when the actions were carried out. Over time, I learned to make the best of everyday life experiences, to be kind but not passive. I made mistakes, but I tried again, I kept learning new things, exploring new opportunities, and growing with each new light. Therefore, I am thankful for these priceless possibilities.

My personal and educational journey has been explored throughout the course of this book: being trapped with work, societal, and family demands, trying to get the equilibrium right. Although the time has been lengthy in starting, writing, and completing this book, I personally feel it finally materialized at a time when it will benefit the right readers. I feel honoured to have had such amazing people in my life who have all helped to form the nucleus of those fascinating experiences.

I nursed the policeman who tried to jail me, missed drowning and I passed my driving test after more than ten attempts. If I had given up with the first failure, I would not be a driver in the UK today neither would I be working as an educator. It may have taken a long time to find workable techniques for holding the trials and testing conversations, but these challenging experiences ended up being the motivational tools that got me to where I am today.

Burnout from experiences and traumas can easily be passed on to others. If I wanted something, I had to work for it, and not all experiences were great, but each had its own lesson. These encounters made me understand what it was like to fail my best paper, to pass with the lowest grades, and even to fail on the paper I thought would have scored the highest mark. The journey was by no means the fastest, but endurance was the key to success.

Growing up on a farm with my parents and siblings is something I did not appreciate until I moved to pastures new. The belief was that I had an excellent relationship with my father, but this did not take away the guilt when he died. I thought I was grateful, but I did not know the true meaning and impact of gratefulness and appreciation until my father passed away. Death is the final journey; until then, everyone can keep aiming for their goals.

Since becoming an educator, reflecting on my role has impacted hugely on my teaching and learning journey. I am more confident about those aspects that enable me to give students the best experience I can offer. This is in addition to keeping in line with a participatory pedagogy approach to always seek ways to develop in my own learning as well. I believe this is crucial if I am going to achieve my goal to reach the students I work with to build that engagement experience. Although, it is challenging at times to get every student started on the right academic track, it is always worth a try, just as someone did for me. For those who are struggling academically and otherwise I would say never give up on yourself. The students who struggle the most and pass in the end are the biggest stars in my crown.

If everyone who reads this book finds at least one benefit that can impact their life in a positive way, that will be success for me. It is my belief that there may be others who have faced their own situations, and through this book, they may find hope. The principal's math question changed my life forever. If I were still believing in my dreams rather than believing in myself, I would probably still be dreaming about being an educator rather than being an educator and fellow of the Higher Education Academy today. Life would be stagnant without motivation.

ABOUT THE AUTHOR

I was born to my parents, Terry and Kenneth Wilson, in the cool hills of Durham, Portland, Jamaica. I was the fifth of nine siblings. My toddler years I cannot remember, but my preschool years are still vivid in my mind. It is interesting to reflect on my past experiences, the sweet memories, the challenges, the triumphs, and the learning experiences as seen through my current lenses.

My education included attending the following training institutions:

- Cooper's Hill All-Age School
- Titchfield High School

- Durham College, Stony Hill Heart Academy
- College of Arts Science and Technology (now University of Technology)
- Excelsior Community College
- Kingston School of Nursing
- Buckinghamshire University
- West London University

Qualifications:

- MA in education
- postgraduate certificate in education
- certificate in management
- diploma, nursing studies
- BSc honours nursing
- RN
- RHMN
- registered practice educator/lecturer
- teacher of the Nursing and Midwifery Council
- fellow of the Higher Education Academy

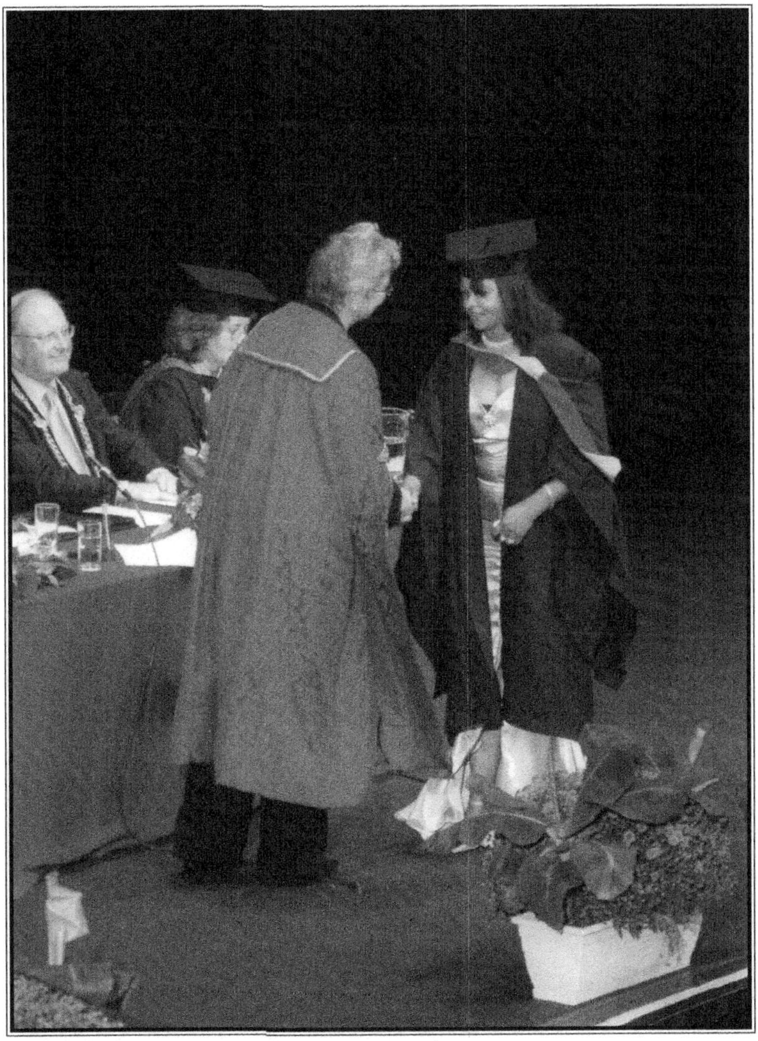

Printed in Great Britain
by Amazon